THE USBORNE
INTERNET-LINKED
LIBRARY OF SCIENCE
ANIMAL
WORLD

Close-up view
of a fish's scales

First published in 2001 by Usborne Publishing Ltd,
Usborne House, 83-85 Saffron Hill, London EC1N 8RT, England.

www.usborne.com

THE USBORNE
INTERNET-LINKED
LIBRARY OF SCIENCE
ANIMAL WORLD

Laura Howell, Kirsteen Rogers
and Corinne Henderson

Designed by Karen Tomlins, Jane Rigby,
Candice Whatmore and Adam Constantine

Digital illustrations by Verinder Bhachu
Digital imagery by Joanne Kirkby

Edited by Laura Howell

Cover design: Cristina Adami

Consultants: Dr Margaret Rostron and Dr John Rostron

Web site adviser: Lisa Watts
Editorial assistant: Valerie Modd

Managing designer: Ruth Russell
Managing editor: Judy Tatchell

INTERNET LINKS

Throughout this book, we have suggested Web sites where you can find out more about animals. Here are some of the things you can do on the Web sites:

- watch animals in Africa via a live Web cam
- look at the different parts of animals' bodies through a powerful electron microscope
- dissect a virtual frog, then reassemble it
- get the latest news on endangered species
- take a tour of a rainforest

USBORNE QUICKLINKS

To visit the sites in this book, go to the Usborne Quicklinks Web site, where you'll find links to take you to all the sites. Just go to **www.usborne-quicklinks.com** and enter the keywords "science animals".

The links in Usborne Quicklinks are regularly reviewed and updated, but occasionally you may get a message that a site is unavailable. This might be temporary, so try again later, or even the next day. If any of the sites close down, we will, if possible, replace them with suitable alternatives, so you will always find an up-to-date list of sites in Usborne Quicklinks.

WHAT YOU NEED

Some Web sites need additional free programs, called plug-ins, to play sounds, or to show videos, animations or 3-D images. A message will appear on your screen if a site needs a particular plug-in. There is usually a button on the site that you can click on to download it. Alternatively, go to **www.usborne-quicklinks.com** and click on "Net Help". There you can find links to download plug-ins.

www.usborne-quicklinks.com

Go to Usborne Quicklinks and enter the keywords "science animals" for:

- direct links to all the Web sites in this book
- free downloadable pictures, which appear throughout this book marked with a ★ symbol

INTERNET SAFETY

When using the Internet, please make sure you follow these guidelines:

- Ask your parent's or guardian's permission before you connect to the Internet.

- If a Web site asks you to enter your name, address, e-mail address, telephone number or any other personal details, ask permission from an adult before you type anything.

- If you receive an e-mail from someone you don't know, tell an adult and do not reply to the e-mail.

- Never arrange to meet with anyone you have talked to on the Internet.

NOTES FOR PARENTS

The Web sites described in this book are regularly reviewed and the links in Usborne Quicklinks are updated. However, the content of a Web site may change at any time and Usborne Publishing is not responsible for the content on any Web site other than its own. We recommend that children are supervised while on the Internet, that they do not use Internet Chat Rooms, and that you use Internet filtering software to block unsuitable material. Please ensure that your children read and follow the safety guidelines printed above. For more information, see the "Net Help" area on the Usborne Quicklinks Web site.

DOWNLOADABLE PICTURES

Pictures in this book marked with a ★ symbol may be downloaded from Usborne Quicklinks for your own personal use, for example, to illustrate a homework report or project. The pictures are the copyright of Usborne Publishing and may not be used for any commercial or profit-related purpose.

SEE FOR YOURSELF

The *See for yourself* boxes in this book contain experiments, activities or observations which we have tested. Some recommended Web sites also contain experiments, but we have not tested all of these. This book will be used by readers of different ages and abilities, so it is important that you do not tackle an experiment on your own, either from the book or the Web, that involves equipment that you do not normally use, such as a kitchen knife or cooker. Instead, ask an adult to help you.

CONTENTS

7   Animal world

8   Animal cells

10   Body structure

12   Body coverings

14   Moving in water

16   Flying and gliding

18   Moving on land

20   Feeding

22   Teeth and digestion

24   Breathing

26   Internal balance

28   Sending messages

30   Animal senses

34   Creating new life

38   Life cycles

40   Ecology

42   Food and energy

44   Balance in nature

46   Conservation

48   Evolution

50   Classification

54   Facts and lists

56   A-Z of scientific terms

60   Test yourself

61   Index

64   Acknowledgements

Biologists group together, or classify, animal species based on their physical features. Snakes belong to a group of animals called reptiles. Most reptiles lay eggs, have scaly skin and keep their bodies warm by basking in the Sun.

ANIMAL WORLD

An animal is a living thing which can move, breathe, reproduce and react to the world around it. Animals come in many shapes and sizes, from smaller than a pinhead to larger than a bus, and exist in almost every environment on Earth. This book reveals many aspects of animals' lives, including their different methods of survival, and how they are affected by the human world.

ANIMAL CELLS

Every living thing is made up of one or more tiny units called **cells**. All the processes needed for life, such as producing energy from food and removing waste, take place inside cells.

PARTS OF A CELL

There are many different kinds of cells, each with a particular job to do, but most share certain features.

Cells contain a number of small parts called **organelles**, which have various functions. The largest and most important organelle is the **nucleus**. This controls everything that happens inside the cell. It has a double-layered outer skin, called the **nuclear membrane**, and a gel-like middle.

All cells are surrounded by a protective layer called the **cell membrane**, which holds together the contents of the cell. This layer is semipermeable, which means that it lets some substances pass through it, but not others.

The rest of the cell is called the **cytoplasm**. The cell membrane, nucleus and cytoplasm are collectively called the **protoplasm**.

Cluster of animal cells, shown at many thousand times its real size

Centrioles play a part in cell division.

Ribosomes help to build up substances called **proteins**, which are needed for all functions within the cell.

Lysosomes can destroy invading bacteria* and parts of the cell that are no longer needed.

Organelles in a typical animal cell (not shown to scale)

The **Golgi complex** stores and distributes the substances made inside the cell.

The **nucleolus** makes the ingredients of ribosomes.

Nucleus. The nuclear membrane has channels called **nuclear pores**, which can open and close to let substances in and out of the nucleus.

Mitochondria convert simple substances into energy for the cell.

Vacuoles are small, temporary sacs in the cytoplasm. They are used as storage areas for liquids or fats.

The **endoplasmic reticulum** is a series of channels used to transport materials around the cell.

* Bacteria, 51.

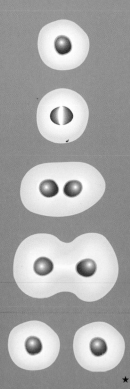

These cells are growing and dividing. Many cells reproduce themselves to allow growth and to replace cells that wear out naturally.

CELL DIVISION

Cells are constantly dying or wearing out, so new ones need to be made. Cells make copies of themselves by splitting into two identical cells, called **daughter cells**.

Stages of cell divison

This single cell is about to start dividing.

The nuclear membrane disappears and the contents of the nucleus begin to pull apart.

The contents reform as two identical nuclei.

A **cleavage furrow** forms, cutting through the middle of the cell.

The cleavage furrow cuts through the cell. Two daughter cells are formed.

★

BUILDING WITH CELLS

Different cell types have different functions. This is called **specialization**. Animal cells come in a variety of shapes and sizes, depending on their job.

Cells of the same type combine to form **tissue**. For example, **columnar epithelial cells** are long and column-shaped, and allow substances to pass through them. They group together to make a tissue called **epithelium**. This is ideal for lining organs such as intestines, because gases and liquids can pass through it easily.

Columnar epithelial cells

Nucleus   Cytoplasm

Several different types of tissue together form an **organ**, such as the stomach or intestines.

Epithelial cells   Muscle cells

Cells group together

Epithelial tissue   Muscle tissue

Tissues combine to form the wall of the intestine.

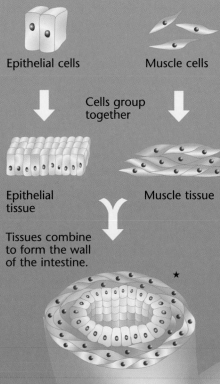
★

SYSTEMS

A group of organs which does a particular job is known as a **system**. For example, an animal's **digestive system** breaks down its food into simpler substances. The digestive system of the frog below contains four main organs: the stomach, liver, pancreas and intestine.

Organs in a frog's digestive system

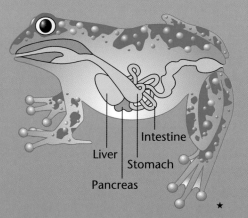

Intestine

Liver

Stomach

Pancreas

★

A frog has other systems, including a **skeletal system**, which supports its body, and a **circulatory system**, which transports blood around it. All the systems together make up a living individual called an **organism**, in this case a frog.

BODY STRUCTURE

The structure of living creatures varies greatly. Animals with the simplest body structure are made of a single cell. More complex creatures are **multicellular**, which means that their bodies are made of hundreds, or even millions, of cells. Most animals have a fluid-filled body cavity and a skeleton.

The body of this starfish is made up of many parts. Its main organs are in the middle.

SIMPLE BODIES

Single-celled amoeba

Simple creatures have a **unicellular** structure. This means that their bodies are made up of a single cell. Some carry out processes common to all animals, such as feeding and moving. The internal parts of many, such as amoebas, are not fixed in place, but move around as the organism changes shape.

SEGMENTED BODIES

The bodies of some animals, such as worms and centipedes, are divided into separate areas called **segments**. A worm's segments are called **metameres**. Each one is almost identical. Segmentation of this type is called **metameric segmentation**. Walls of muscle tissue, each one called a **septum**, divide one metamere from the next.

Earthworm

Simplified cutaway view

Metamere

Septum

Parts of worm's nervous system can be seen in each segment.

Divisions between segments can be seen on the body's surface.

DIVIDED BODIES

Some more complex creatures, such as insects, have a segmented body structure, but the segmentation is not always clearly visible. Their bodies are divided into three parts: the **head**, **thorax** and **abdomen**. Each part is made up of a group of segments called **tagmata**. Unlike metameres, tagmata do not have dividing walls.

Body structure of a wasp

Head (carries main sense organs)

Thorax (upper body area, contains flight muscles)

Abdomen (contains most of insect's body organs)

Most insects have two pairs of wings and three pairs of legs, arranged symmetrically on either side of their thorax.

Paired legs (attached to thorax)

Wings (attached to thorax). This wasp's rear wings are hidden beneath its front wings.

BODY SYMMETRY

Most freely-moving animals have **bilateral symmetry**. This means that one half of their body mirrors the other. Other animals, such as starfish, have **radial symmetry**. This means that there are two or more lines of symmetry, which radiate from one central point.

Bilateral symmetry

Radial symmetry

Only one division can produce two identical halves.

Many lines of symmetry produce identical halves.

BODY CAVITIES

Almost all animals have a fluid-filled body cavity called a **perivisceral cavity**, which acts as a cushion for the internal organs. Two types of perivisceral cavity are the coelom and the haemocoel.

A **coelom** is filled with fluid and contained by a membrane called the **peritoneum**.

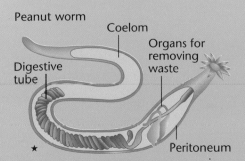

Peanut worm

Coelom

Organs for removing waste

Digestive tube

★

Peritoneum

A **haemocoel** is a cavity filled with blood. It forms part of the animal's blood system.

Spider

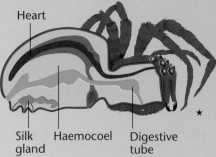

Heart

Silk gland

Haemocoel

Digestive tube

★

SKELETONS

A **skeleton** provides support for an animal's body, and protects its internal organs from damage. It helps the animal to move, by providing a surface for its muscles to pull on. There are three kinds of skeleton, described below.

An **endoskeleton** is a hard framework inside an animal's body. Endoskeletons are usually made of bone, but in **cartilaginous fish**, such as sharks and rays, they are made of a flexible substance called **cartilage**.

A rabbit's endoskeleton

An **exoskeleton** is a hard body covering which supports and protects an animal with no internal skeleton. Crabs and insects are animals with an exoskeleton.

A crab's exoskeleton includes claws and leg coverings.

A **hydrostatic skeleton** is a system in which the fluid-filled body cavity provides pressure for muscles in the body wall to work against. Animals such as sea anemones, which have no hard framework for support, have hydrostatic skeletons.

A sea anemone's body is like a soft bag made up of two layers of tissue with a watery gel in between.

A sea anemone takes in water through its mouth. When the mouth shuts, its body becomes firm and solid, like a water-filled balloon.

Internet links

Go to **www.usborne-quicklinks.com** for links to the following Web sites:

Web site 1 Find out about worms, including their body structure.

Web site 2 Cockroach body structure.

Web sites 3–5 Detailed and fascinating information on the body structure of insects, birds and mammals.

Web site 6 Dissect a virtual frog to see its skeleton and organs.

Web site 7 Put your dissected frog back together again.

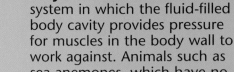

11

BODY COVERINGS

All creatures have an outer layer to enclose their bodies. Some animals have a layer of skin, covered with feathers or fur. Others have a hard covering of some kind. In some cases, this covering also provides support for the animal's body.

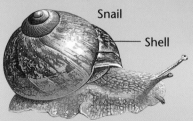

A pangolin's body is covered with thick, sharp-edged scales. These stick out to defend it from enemies.

WATERPROOFING

Many soft-bodied animals have a waterproof outer layer called a **cuticle**, which is produced by the skin. In some animals, such as earthworms, the cuticle stays soft and waxy. In others, especially arthropods*, the cuticle hardens to form a supportive outer framework or **exoskeleton**.

An arthropod's cuticle prevents its body from drying out. It is tough, but also light enough to allow flight, for example in insects. It is made up of sections called **sclerites**, joined by flexible membranes. This arrangement allows the creature to move freely.

The ridged sections on an ant's body are its sclerites.

Sclerite

See for yourself

Look at a woodlouse under a magnifying lens. As it moves around, notice its sclerites. If it is alarmed, it may curl its flexible body into a ball. After you have finished looking at it, return the animal to where you found it.

Woodlouse

NEW COATS

A lot of animals shed their coverings in order to grow. An arthropod sheds its cuticle when it grows too big for it, and a new, larger one forms. This process is called **ecdysis**.

Crustaceans, such as crabs, have a protective cuticle which they shed. This hard, shield-like "shell" is called a **carapace**.

This crab's new hard covering, or carapace, is fully hardened.

Some other animals have a carapace which is not made of cuticle, and is not shed. Turtles and tortoises, for instance, are born with a carapace made of bony plates fused together, covered with a layer of horn. The carapace is connected to their body at the ribs, spine, shoulders and hips. As the animal grows, each plate in its carapace grows too.

Tortoise   Carapace

Snails and other molluscs have a protective body covering called a **shell**. This is formed from a substance secreted by the animal's body. Like a tortoise's carapace, the shell grows with the animal and is not shed.

Snail

Shell

PROTECTIVE PLATES

Some animals are covered in hard plates called **scuta**. These can be made of horn, bone, or a substance called **chitin**. Scuta help to keep the animal safe from predators.

This armadillo's bony scuta are covered with horn.

* Arthropods, 52.

PRICKLY PROTECTION

Some mammals, such as porcupines and hedgehogs, have prickly body coverings made of **keratin**. This is the main ingredient of your hair and nails. The animal uses its prickles for protection.

When threatened, this porcupine raises its prickles, called **quills**, as a warning. If attacked, it moves backwards, stabbing the predator with its quills.

SCALY CREATURES

Many animals have a mosaic of **scales** covering their bodies. Scales tend to be thinner than scuta, and are often made from different substances. Many reptiles, for example, have scales made from hardened skin. Scuta are usually horny or bony, and are heavier than scales.

A butterfly's wings are protected by tiny overlapping scales made of chitin. These loose, powdery scales are very fragile, and can rub off if touched. Underneath their scaly coverings, the wings are thin and transparent, like those of a fly.

Close-up of a butterfly's wing

You can see a butterfly's scales under an ordinary microscope.

Small tortoiseshell butterfly

FISH SCALES

There are two main types of fish scales: dermal and placoid. **Dermal scales** are small, bony plates embedded in the skin. They grow out of a tough lower layer of skin called the **dermis**, and are covered by a thinner, slimy layer called the **epidermis**. Fish with bone skeletons have dermal scales.

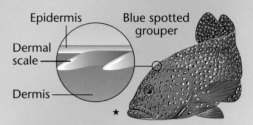

Epidermis

Blue spotted grouper

Dermal scale

Dermis

★

Placoid scales, also called **denticles**, are sharp, backward-pointing scales, which stick out from the skin. Cartilaginous fish*, such as sharks and rays, have placoid scales.

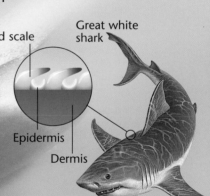

Placoid scale

Great white shark

Epidermis

Dermis

★

Internet links

Go to **www.usborne-quicklinks.com** for links to the following Web sites:

Web site 1 Browse the Boston Museum of Science Image Gallery for black and white electron microscope pictures of different body coverings.

Web site 2 Look at amazing close-up pictures of dogfish and butterfly scales.

Web site 3 See a selection of animal images at the London Natural History Museum. You can type in the name of any animal to search for it.

Web site 4 Learn all about feathers and their unique structure.

* Cartilaginous fish, 11.

13

MOVING IN WATER

Most animals are capable of moving from place to place at some stage during their lives. This is called **locomotion**. Many animals have a particular body shape or specialized body parts which help them to move around. For example, some creatures that live in water have flippers or fins.

The caudal fin (tail fin) propels the body forwards.

Anal fin. In some species, this is called the ventral fin.

A fish uses its fins to control balance and direction.

FALSE FEET

Some single-celled organisms, such as amoebas, do not have individual body parts for locomotion. Instead, they form extensions of their bodies called **pseudopodia** (meaning "false feet") which help them to move.

How an amoeba moves

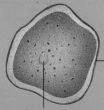

Nucleus

Ectoplasm (outer, rigid cytoplasm*) thins out at one point.

Inner, fluid cytoplasm flows forward to form pseudopodium.

Rest of organism flows forward.

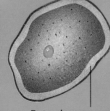

Ectoplasm evens out around the edge.

SIMPLE MOVEMENT

Many microscopic organisms are covered with tiny hairs called **cilia**. These flick back and forth like oars to "row" the creature through the water. Organisms with cilia are known as **ciliates**.

Paramecium

Cilia

Some organisms have long, fine body threads called **flagellae**. These lash to and fro like whips to produce movement. An organism with flagellae is described as a **flagellate**.

Trichomonas

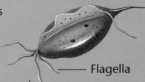

Flagella

All species of bristleworms have paired projections called **parapodia** along the sides of their bodies. These are used for swimming. Each parapodium ends in bristles called **chaetae**.

Ragworm (type of bristleworm)

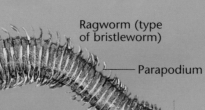

Parapodium

JET PROPELLED

Some animals, including squid, octopuses and jellyfish, move around by jet propulsion. Squid and octupuses do this by taking in water and forcing it out of their body through a funnel-shaped tube called a **hyponome**. The force of this water pushes the animal in the opposite direction.

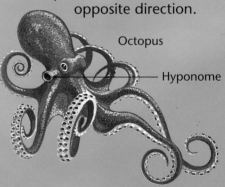

Octopus

Hyponome

Jellyfish move by filling their bell-like bodies with water, then forcing it out. A jellyfish does this several times, moving itself up, and then drifts slowly down.

Jellyfish fills its hollow body with water.

Water is pushed out and the jellyfish moves.

* Cytoplasm, 8.

Dorsal fin

The dorsal fin and anal fin control changes of direction from side to side, and prevent rolling.

Pectoral fin

Pelvic fin

FLIPPERS

Many animals, including some mammals and birds, are well suited to life in the water. They usually have a streamlined shape, and specialized body parts which allow them to swim. Animals such as dolphins, for example, have broad, paddle-like front limbs called **flippers**.

Dolphin

Penguins look clumsy on the land, but they are fantastic swimmers. Their flat, stiff wings are not suitable for flying, but are just the right shape to act as flippers in the water. A penguin can steer under water using its tail and webbed feet.

TYPES OF FINS

All fish have a number of projections called **fins**, which are used as stabilizers, and also to change direction. Fins are supported by fan-shaped **rays**. These are rods of bone or a tough, flexible substance called cartilage. Fish have two sets of fins: median and paired.

Median fins lie in a line down the middle of the fish's back or belly. They are divided into the **dorsal**, **caudal** (tail) and **anal** (or **ventral**) **fins**, shown in the picture above. **Paired fins** (**pectoral** and **pelvic**) stick out sideways from the body. They control movement up or down.

POUCHES OF AIR

Some fish with bone skeletons have a long, air-filled pouch called a **swim bladder** inside their bodies. The fish can control the amount of air inside the bladder, so the density of its body can always be the same as that of the water. This means that the fish does not sink if it stops swimming.

Swim bladder

Fish with cartilage skeletons, such as rays, do not have swim bladders. Their bodies are denser than the water, so they must control their position by other means.

These penguins' streamlined bodies allow them to glide quickly and easily through the water.

See for yourself

When you next see fish in a tank, look at how they use their pelvic fins. Many move them in a figure-of-eight shape. This helps them to swim very smoothly through the water.

Swimming manta ray

Internet links

Go to **www.usborne-quicklinks.com** for links to the following Web sites:

Web site 1 A browseable site containing information about many water animals.

Web site 2 Watch video clips of swimming penguins at Bristol Zoo, England.

Web site 3 Watch video clips of seals, download a Seal Screensaver, or read the Seal Factfile.

Web site 4 Find out how sharks swim.

Web site 5 Lots of information on how animals are adapted for movement in water.

15

FLYING AND GLIDING

Flying allows animals to escape from enemies on the ground, find new sources of food and, in some cases, travel long distances to find a partner. Only creatures with well-developed wings, such as bats, birds and insects, are able to fly, but some animals are able to glide for shorter distances.

This bat's leathery wings are made of skin, stretched over its arms and huge fingers.

Bats are the only mammals that can fly.

BIRDS AND FLIGHT

Birds that fly have many features to help them. These include smooth, light feathers, powerful wings and hollow bones.

BIRD BONES

Many birds have hollow bones, supported by thin, criss-cross structures. These make their bones strong as well as light.

Cross section of a bird's bone

FLIGHT MUSCLES

A bird's wings are attached to a large extension of its breastbone called the **keel**. They are joined by two pairs of large **pectoralis muscles**. These are used to move the wings.

Pectoralis muscles

Cutaway picture of an owl

Keel

FEATHERS

A bird's body and wings are covered with **feathers**. Each one is made up of a central **shaft**, with rows of thread-like **barbs** on either side. Tiny, hooked **barbules** lock the barbs together, creating a flat surface called a **vane**.

Structure of a feather

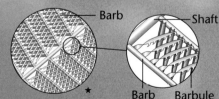

Barb

Shaft

Barb   Barbule

Contour feathers cover the bird's body, giving it a smooth and streamlined shape. **Flight feathers**, also called **remiges**, are long and stiff. They give the wing a large surface area, which is essential for flying.

Flight feathers

The wing can rotate freely at the shoulder, allowing a wide range of movement.

Nerve endings at the base of each feather can detect tiny changes in air currents.

Contour feathers

Gull in flight

FLYING INSECTS

Like birds, insects have light bodies and powerful muscles for flying. However, an insect's body is very large in relation to its thin wings, so it needs much more power than a bird to fly. Energy is stored in the insect's muscles, and is released rapidly as it flies.

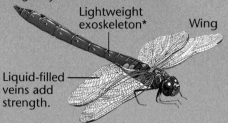

Dragonfly

Lightweight exoskeleton*

Wing

Liquid-filled veins add strength.

Some insects, such as dragonflies, use two pairs of wings to fly. Many insects only use one pair, the other being modified in some way. For example, a beetle's front wings, called **elytra**, form a hard, protective casing made of hardened cuticle* for its rear wings.

Cockchafer beetle

Protective wing cases (elytra)

GLIDERS

Several animals have "flying" as part of their name, but they have no wings, so they cannot actually fly. Instead, they use a variety of methods to glide through the air.

The colugo on the right, for example, has flaps of skin between its front and hind legs. When it jumps, it spreads its limbs like wings. It moves its legs and tail to change direction as it glides from tree to tree.

A flying lizard stretches out its long ribs to form broad, stiff flaps on either side of its body. When the lizard is resting, these flaps fold away against its body.

A colugo gliding through the air

This flying lizard can glide up to 15m between trees.

Flying snakes live in rainforests. They climb trees and can glide up to 50m between branches. A flying snake does this by spreading out its ribcage, making its body into a flattened shape. As it glides, it twists its body through the air in S-shaped movements.

Flying snake

See for yourself

Stroke a feather from top to bottom. It will become ruffled as its barbs unhook. If you stroke the feather in the opposite direction, the barbs will join together to make the feather perfectly smooth again.

Internet links

Go to **www.usborne-quicklinks.com** for links to the following Web sites:

Web site 1 Plenty of fascinating facts about birds and flight, suitable for younger readers.

Web site 2 Visit the Hooper Natural History Museum to find out about flight in birds, insects, dragonflies and prehistoric flying creatures.

Web site 3 Useful information about flight in birds, insects and bats.

Web site 4 Share the lives of a pair of Northern Barred owls, as seen through a camera in their nest box.

Web site 5 Beautiful microscope images of feathers, with facts about their structure and use.

* Cuticle, 12; Exoskeleton, 11.

MOVING ON LAND

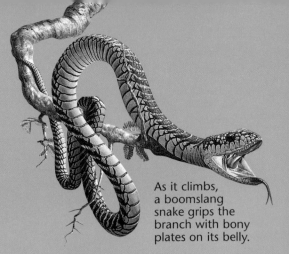

Animals that spend most or all of their lives on land are called **terrestrial animals**. They have many ways of moving around. Most of them use one or more pairs of legs to move. Animals without limbs, such as worms and snakes, move by changing the shapes of their muscular bodies.

As it climbs, a boomslang snake grips the branch with bony plates on its belly.

CRAWLING

Earthworms, and some other soft-bodied creatures, move using muscles in the body wall. Fluid in the body provides pressure for the muscles to work against. As they expand and contract, different parts of the body move forwards.

How an earthworm moves

The movement of the muscles looks like a wave rippling along the body.

A snake has ribs and powerful muscles along the whole length of its body. Most snakes move by stretching forward and pushing back in S-shaped curves. Bony scuta* (plates) on their bellies help them to grip.

CREEPING

Some caterpillars move by arching their bodies, then stretching forwards. Only one end of the body moves forwards at a time, while the legs at the other end grip the surface. This is called **looping**.

How a caterpillar loops

Back legs grip the ground, and front of body stretches forwards.

Front legs grip the ground, and back of body moves forwards. This pulls body into tight arch.

*

SWINGING

Many jungle-dwelling primates*, such as gibbons and orang-utans, can climb or swing using their long, strong front limbs and curved gripping fingers. Most primates can also grip well with their toes.

Some primates have a very flexible tail which can be used like an arm, to grip branches. A tail that can grip is called a **prehensile tail**.

A black-handed spider monkey's tail is strong enough to support its whole body.

A cheetah's claws grip the ground like spiked running shoes.

Powerful muscles and a flexible body help the cheetah to move fast.

* Scuta, 12; Primates, 52.

USING LEGS

An animal's limbs are arranged symmetrically on either side of its body, and front limbs may look different from back limbs. Animals that walk upright on two legs, such as birds, are called **bipeds**. Most bipeds move one leg forwards with every step, but some birds hop on both legs.

Ostriches have extremely strong legs and they can run very fast.

A four-legged animal is called a **quadruped**. Typically, when walking, diagonally opposite legs move together, for example front left and rear right.

When running fast, most mammals stretch out their front and rear legs and then bring them together in powerful bounding movements.

Creatures with six legs, such as insects, are called **hexapods**. When walking, one leg on one side of the body and two legs on the other side move forwards.

Circles show which of the ladybird's legs move together.

Many-legged creatures, called **myriapods**, can have up to 750 legs. These move in wave-like motions along the body.

LEAPING

Some creatures, such as frogs and fleas, can leap huge distances. They do this using powerful muscles in their back legs. Some other creatures, such as the springtail below, have different body parts which allow them to leap.

How a springtail leaps

Tail is folded under the body.   Tail is quickly flicked onto the ground.   Springtail is pushed into the air.

STANCE

Stance is the word which describes how an animal stands and moves. It is determined by the part of the foot on which the animal stands.

Unguligrade animals, such as horses, walk on hooves at the tips of the toes.

Digitigrade animals, such as dogs, walk on the undersides of the toes.

Plantigrade animals, such as bears, walk on the underside of the whole foot.

★

See for yourself

Look at different animals, and notice how many legs they have and what part of their feet they walk on. Also, do the animals move their legs differently when they are walking and running?

Internet links

Go to **www.usborne-quicklinks.com** for links to the following Web sites:

Web site 1 Watch Web cams of African wildlife.

Web site 2 Read about the features that enable a cheetah to be the fastest mammal on Earth.

Web site 3 Explore the Lincoln Park Zoo in America to see how different animals move.

Web site 4 Fascinating facts about monkeys and other primates, including how they move.

Web site 5 An in-depth look at mammal locomotion.

This Thompson's gazelle can run at up to 80 kilometres per hour.

FEEDING

The structure of an animal's mouthparts depends on the kind of food it eats. Teeth, and the part they play in feeding, are described on page 22. Toothless creatures, called **edentates**, often have a beak or a flexible tongue for capturing their food.

A sea anemone's mouth (not visible here) is in the middle of its body.

SIMPLE FEEDING

Single-celled organisms, such as amoebas, do not have mouths. Instead, they feed by a process called **phagocytosis**. Their bodies flow around and engulf tiny food particles. The food is then digested in a chemical-filled area called a **vacuole**.

How an amoeba feeds

Amoeba flows around food particle.

Particle is surrounded by amoeba.

Amoeba begins to break down particle.

★

FEEDING IN WATER

Many animals **filter feed**, by sieving small creatures out of the water. Barnacles do this using bristly limbs called **cirri**.

Cirri

Barnacles

Some whales feed using frayed plates of whalebone, called **baleen**, which hang down from their top jaw. Small animals called krill get caught in the baleen.

Baleen

Water and food in

Water out

★

Cross section of a tentacle

Cnidoblast

Nematocyst shoots out.

Cnidarians*, such as sea anemones, have tiny sac-like cells called **cnidoblasts** or **thread cells** on their tentacles for seizing food. Each cnidoblast contains a long, poisonous thread called a **nematocyst**. When a tentacle touches something, the threads shoot out to sting and paralyse it. The tentacles then pull the prey into the animal's mouth.

SCRAPERS

Almost all molluscs*, such as snails, have a rough tongue called a **radula**. It is used like a file to scrape plant matter into the animal's mouth. If you listen closely to a feeding snail, you may hear its radula scraping.

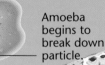

Position of radula

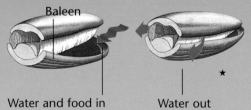

Grey whale filtering water

* Cnidarians, Molluscs, 52.

INSECT MOUTHPARTS

Insects' mouths are made up of a number of different parts: the mandibles, maxillae, labrum and labium. The appearance of these mouthparts varies from species to species.

A grasshopper's mouthparts

★

Hypopharynx (tongue) used for sucking up liquids. It is not visible here.

Labrum (upper lip) covers and protects other mouthparts.

Mandibles are used for holding or biting.

Maxillae usually help to push food into the mouth.

Palps are used to taste food.

Labium (lower lip) is also used to push food into the mouth.

The labium of a housefly is an extended pad-like sucking organ. The fly dissolves its food using saliva, then mops up the liquid with its spongy mouthparts.

Food is taken in through grooves in the fly's labium.

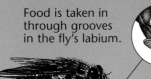

In some insects, the maxillae fit together to make a long tube called a **proboscis**. Female mosquitoes have a sharp, rigid proboscis for piercing skin. A butterfly has a flexible proboscis for sucking nectar from flowers.

Butterfly

Proboscis

Flamingos feed with their heads upside down in the water.

The flamingo's beak acts like a scoop, taking in water, mud and tiny plants and animals.

BEAKS

A bird's hard upper and lower jaws come together to form a **beak** or **bill**. The shape and size of a bird's beak depend on the kind of food it eats.

Types of beaks

A wood warbler's thin, sharp beak catches insects.

A kestrel's sharp, curved beak tears meat.

A honey-eater's long, thin beak sucks from flowers.

A greenfinch's strong, chunky beak cracks seeds.

A teal's flattish bill scoops up water plants.

A heron's long, sharp beak stabs fish.

Cross section of a flamingo's mouthparts

Spikes for capturing food

Spikes on tongue scrape food off beak.

Flamingos have unusual beaks and tongues for sieving food. They feed by raking their beaks through the mud at the bottom of lakes. Tiny plants and animals stick to small spikes on the inside of the beak. The flamingo scrapes the food off its beak using larger spikes on its tongue.

Internet links

Go to **www.usborne-quicklinks.com** for links to the following Web sites:

Web site 1 Read about different species competing for food in the "Animal Olympics". You can judge which "athlete" should win the gold!

Web site 2 Pictures, information and interesting facts about many types of bird beaks and tongues.

Web site 3 Find out about grey whales, and discover how they use their baleen to feed.

Web site 4 Amazing electron microscope images of various insects' heads and mouthparts.

TEETH AND DIGESTION

Many animals have **teeth** to tear, chew or grind their food. Animals with teeth are described as **dentate**. After it is swallowed, an animal's food is broken down further by the **digestive system**, so it can be absorbed by the body. Animals have different sorts of teeth and digestive systems depending on the type of food they eat.

Like many plant eaters, a giraffe has flat, ridged teeth for grinding plants.

MEAT EATERS

Meat-eating animals, called **carnivores**, have sharp teeth for tearing meat. Dagger-like **canines** are used for piercing and killing prey. The large, jagged **carnassials** are used for slicing meat. Smaller front teeth called **incisors** come together to bite or scrape meat from bones.

Sharks' teeth grow in rows in their jaws. When they lose a tooth from the front set, another moves forwards to take its place. Almost all mammals have two sets of teeth during their lifetimes. The second set, called **permanent teeth**, cannot be replaced if lost.

This picture of a lioness shows the teeth of a carnivore.

Carnassials slide against each other to slice flesh.

Canines stab and pierce flesh.

Incisors scrape meat from bone.

PLANT EATERS

Plant-eating animals, called **herbivores**, have square cheek teeth (**premolars** and **molars**), for grinding plants. The incisors are long and chisel-shaped. In ruminants, such as cows and deer, these grip plants against a hard pad in the top jaw. A gap called the **diastema**, between the incisors and cheek teeth, allows space to move the tongue.

This deer's skull shows the teeth of a herbivore.

Incisors

Incisors press against this pad to bite and grip.

Diastema

Cheek teeth have ridged tops for grinding.

ALL-PURPOSE TEETH

Animals that eat both plants and meat are called **omnivores**. An omnivore's teeth can be many different shapes and sizes, depending on the kind of food it eats. For instance, a monkey has long canines to pierce flesh, and flat back teeth to grind plants.

This monkey's skull shows an omnivore's varied types of teeth.

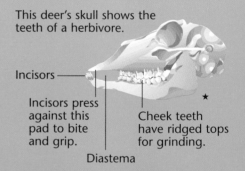

DIGESTING PLANTS

Plants contain a tough substance called **cellulose**, which is hard to digest. Herbivores therefore have more complex digestive organs than other animals. Most herbivores have a sac inside their body called a **caecum**, in which plant matter is broken down by bacteria*.

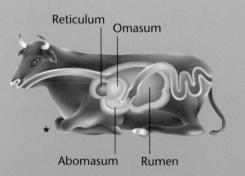

Position of caecum in rabbit

Ruminants, such as cows, sheep and deer, have four stomach-like chambers to digest their food: the rumen, reticulum, omasum and abomasum.

Digestive system of a cow

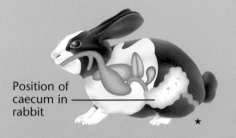

Reticulum
Omasum
Abomasum
Rumen

First, food passes unchewed into the **rumen**. There, bacteria start to break down cellulose. The partially-digested food is processed in the second chamber, or **reticulum**. It is then returned to the mouth to be re-chewed. Food at this stage is called the **cud**.

After chewing, the food is swallowed for a second time, and then broken down further in the remaining chambers, the **omasum** and the **abomasum** (true stomach).

Bacteria, 51.

DIGESTION IN BIRDS

Birds have no teeth to break up their food, so they have a digestive system specially designed to deal with solids.

After food has been swallowed, it is stored in a thin-walled pouch called the **crop**. It then travels to a thick, muscular-walled pouch called the **gizzard**. Here, the food is ground up by muscular ridges on the gizzard walls and small stones which the bird has swallowed.

Meat-eating birds, such as owls and hawks, swallow their prey whole. The parts which cannot be digested, such as bones and fur, form a compact **pellet** inside the bird's stomach. This is coughed back up and put out through the mouth.

Crop

Gizzard

Waste is stored in a chamber called the **cloaca**, before being passed out of the bird's body.

This pellet came from a barn owl. An owl pellet may contain the skeletons of several small animals.

Bone

4-6cm

Owls eat small animals, such as frogs and mice, in one piece.

See for yourself

Next time you are in a wooded area, look for bird pellets. Use a stick to turn them over, and see what they are made up of. You are most likely to find pellets under trees and other places where birds roost. You can use a magnifying glass to look closely, but never touch a pellet with your hands.

Bone from inside a pellet

Internet links

Go to **www.usborne-quicklinks.com** for links to the following Web sites:

Web site 1 This site has an excellent database of animal facts, including information on their diets.

Web site 2 Find out about sharks' teeth.

Web site 3 Examine the teeth of dozens of animals.

Web site 4 Useful facts about owls and owl pellets.

Web site 5 Fascinating information on many animals' feeding habits.

BREATHING

Animals breathe in oxygen from air or water. They use it to release energy from digested food, breathing out carbon dioxide as a waste product. The process by which gases pass in and out of the body is known as **gaseous exchange**. This takes place in the **respiratory organs**. Gases travel to and from these organs in the blood.

BREATHING IN WATER

Most water-dwelling animals take in oxygen through organs called **gills** or **branchiae**. There are two types of gills – internal and external.

Internal gills are found inside the bodies of many water creatures, especially fish. Most fish have four pairs of gills, with openings called **gill slits** between them. In bony fish, the gills are covered by a bony flap called the **operculum**. In cartilaginous fish*, they are open to the water at all times.

The water which washes over the gills comes in through a fish's mouth, and is pumped out through the gill slits. Each gill is made up of a curved rod called the **gill bar** or **gill arch**, which has many fine **gill filaments** radiating from it.

Each gill filament has even finer **gill lamellae** branching off it, like the branches of a feather. These all contain blood vessels. Oxygen is taken into the blood from the water, and carbon dioxide from the blood passes out to be washed away.

Many other water creatures, such as caddisfly larvae and tadpoles, have **external gills**. These are on the outside of the body. Their exact form depends on the type of animal, but in many cases they are frilly growths behind the head.

Tadpole

Gills

Some simple water creatures have tubes called **siphons**. These carry gases, which are dissolved in water, to and from their gills. A siphon that carries gases to the gills is described as **inhalant**, and one that carries them from the gills is described as **exhalant**.

Breathing with gills

Mouth open

Operculum closed

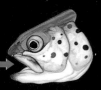

Water in

Mouth closes, operculum opens.

Water forced through gill slits (washing over gill filaments).

* Water forced out between operculum and body wall.

Operculum has been removed to show four gills.

Gill rakers filter out tiny creatures from the water. Not all species have them.

Gill slit

Gill filament

Gill bar

Gill lamellae

Cutaway diagram of a whelk

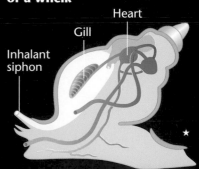

Heart

Gill

Inhalant siphon

*

* Cartilaginous fish, 11.

AMPHIBIANS

Amphibians* can spend time both in water and on land, and take oxygen from water or air. A frog, for instance, does this in a variety of ways. In water, dissolved oxygen passes in through its skin to the blood vessels beneath, and carbon dioxide passes out the same way.

On land, a frog breathes using a pair of light sacs called lungs. Gaseous exchange through the blood vessels inside these lungs works in the same way as in other vertebrate* lungs (see right). They are less efficient, however, because the frog uses a lot of energy actively pumping the gases in and out. So even on land, much gaseous exchange still happens through the skin.

The frog is also able to exchange gases directly through blood vessels in the lining of its mouth.

This frog's skin gleams with natural moisture. Gases dissolve in the moisture and are exchanged through the skin.

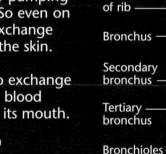

LUNGS

All reptiles, birds and mammals have a pair of **lungs** for exchanging gases. Their breathing is automatic and effortless. Air flows in and out of the lungs through a tube called the **trachea** or **windpipe**. This splits into two thick tubes, each one called a **bronchus**, which in turn branch into smaller **secondary** and **tertiary bronchi** inside the lung.

Tertiary bronchi branch into tiny tubes called **bronchioles**. Each bronchiole ends in a small sac called an **alveolus**. Gases are exchanged through tiny blood vessels on the surface of each alveolus.

Diagram of a mammal's lung

Trachea

Cut end of rib

Bronchus

Secondary bronchus

Tertiary bronchus

Bronchioles

★

HOW INSECTS BREATHE

Gaseous exchange in insects takes place through small holes called **spiracles** in their bodies. Air enters the spiracles, and travels through a network of pipes called **tracheae**. These branch into tiny tubes called **tracheoles**, which carry gases to and from cells in the body.

Respiratory system of a flea

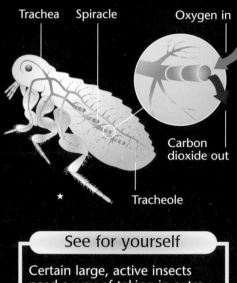

Trachea   Spiracle   Oxygen in

Carbon dioxide out

★   Tracheole

See for yourself

Certain large, active insects need a way of taking in extra oxygen. They do this by opening their spiracles and pumping their abdomen in and out. You may see a grasshopper or a large moth doing this when it is resting.

Internet links

Go to **www.usborne-quicklinks.com** for links to the following Web sites:

Web site 1 How bird and human breathing systems differ.

Web site 2 Find out how bony fishes breathe.

Web site 3 Learn how dolphins breathe.

Web site 4 Read a short and simple article explaining how whales breathe.

Web site 5 Discover how a shark's gills work.

Amphibians, 52; Vertebrates, 32.

INTERNAL BALANCE

In order to stay alive, an animal's temperature must remain within certain limits, and substances in its body, such as salts and water, need to be kept at the right level. Keeping the body and the chemicals inside it in a balanced state is called **homeostasis**. Solid and liquid waste must also be removed. The parts of the body that deal with this are known as the **excretory organs**. In most animals, they include the lungs, skin, liver and kidneys.

BODY TEMPERATURE

An animal cannot survive for long if it is too hot or too cold, because its organs cannot work efficiently. Keeping the body at the right temperature is called **thermoregulation**. The animal's skin and blood usually play an important part in this.

Mammals and birds can keep their body at the same internal temperature in most conditions. They are described as **warm-blooded**. All other animals are **cold-blooded**. This means that their body temperature is not under their internal control, and it changes with the temperature of their surroundings.

WARMING UP

When a warm-blooded animal needs extra heat, its feathers or hairs stand on end. These act like a blanket, trapping warm air next to its skin. The animal may also begin to shiver, which produces heat. Both of these actions happen automatically when an animal's body temperature becomes too low.

Cold-blooded creatures, though, have no way of using their bodies to keep warm. If their temperature is too low, they must bask in the Sun to raise it again.

These young owls have fluffy down feathers, which trap heat next to their bodies.

COOLING DOWN

Cold-blooded animals must find shade or water to cool their bodies. Warm-blooded animals can cool down in other ways. For example, some sweat when they are too hot. The evaporation of moisture from their skin cools them down. A hairy animal that is unable to sweat may pant instead. It loses moisture and heat from the tongue's surface and in air it breathes out. Many desert mammals, like this fennec fox, lose heat through the lining of their huge ears.

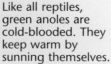

Like all reptiles, green anoles are cold-blooded. They keep warm by sunning themselves.

Fennec fox

WATER BALANCE

All creatures need to keep the amount of water in their bodies at the right level, or their organs will not work properly.

Single-celled creatures, such as Paramecium, do this using a tiny sac in their bodies called a **contractile vacuole**.

Paramecium

Contractile vacuole expands as it fills with water.

At intervals, the vacuole expels its contents.

Birds have large, efficient kidneys, but no bladder. They excrete a solid waste called uric acid.

LIVER AND KIDNEYS

In many animals, most waste is removed from the body by the liver and kidneys. The **liver** breaks down amino acids from food, to produce a substance called **urea**. This is mixed with blood and taken to the **kidneys**. These filter the blood, removing the urea, along with water and harmful salts, which form a liquid called **urine**. This is stored in a sac-like organ called the **bladder**, which is emptied regularly.

Diagram of kidneys and bladder

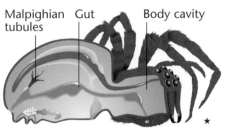

Kidney

The **renal artery** carries blood to the kidneys.

The **renal vein** carries filtered blood away from the kidneys.

Bladder

WASTE TUBES

Arthropods* do not have kidneys or a liver. Instead, they have tubes called **malpighian tubules**. These remove liquid waste from the body cavity (haemocoel*). The waste is turned into solid **uric acid** in the gut. Any water is reabsorbed into the blood. The uric acid leaves the body.

Excretory system of a spider

Malpighian tubules

Gut

Body cavity

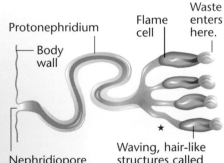

Some soft-bodied creatures, such as simple worms, have waste tubes called **protonephridia**. Waste enters these through hollow **flame cells** and leaves the body through tiny holes called **nephridiopores**.

Protonephridium

Flame cell

Waste enters here.

Body wall

Nephridiopore

Waving, hair-like structures called cilia draw waste in.

Internet links

Go to **www.usborne-quicklinks.com** for links to the following Web sites:

Web site 1 How cold-blooded, warm-blooded, feathered and furry animals survive in the Antarctic.

Web site 2 Weird and wonderful facts about how some frogs deal with extreme temperatures.

Web site 3 More strange facts about how some frogs change colour when the temperature changes.

Web site 4 Watch a short animated movie and take a quiz about how the kidneys work.

* Arthropods, 52; Haemocoel, 11.

SENDING MESSAGES

The process of giving information that another creature can understand is called **communication**. Animals communicate with each other in many ways, using colours, sounds, movements and chemicals. Most of their messages are connected with finding a mate or giving a warning to other animals.

A skunk growls, stamps its feet and raises its tail to warn enemies to leave it alone, or it will spray a smelly liquid at them.

COLOUR CODING

Many animals respond to particular patterns or colours. A male European robin, for example, will become aggressive when a rival shows its red breast near its territory. A display like this that triggers a certain response is called a **sign stimulus**.

European robin displaying red breast

Creatures which are foul-tasting, poisonous, or have a painful sting or bite, often have brightly coloured bodies. Predators quickly learn to avoid any animals with these bright colours.

This cinnabar caterpillar's black and yellow stripes warn that it is poisonous.

A male frigate bird's throat sac is usually orange, but during the mating season it turns red and can be puffed out.

Some harmless animals have similar colours to poisonous ones. Predators think that these animals are dangerous and leave them alone. This copy-cat colouration is called **mimicry**.

Swallowtail butterfly

African monarch butterfly

Birds will not eat the non-poisonous swallowtail, because they mistake it for the poisonous African monarch.

Animals often display coloured body parts to attract a mate. For instance, a male frigate bird inflates his bright red throat sac to attract females. He also snaps his bill and holds his body in different poses.

The frigate bird sits on a nest of sticks as he displays. If a female is interested, she offers him more sticks.

The males of many other bird species, such as peacocks, develop fantastic plumage during the mating season. They raise their feathers and shiver them in a dazzling display.

BODY LANGUAGE

Many animals, especially those that live in groups, give out messages by the way they move or hold their bodies. Bees, for example, move in particular patterns, or **dances**, to show where food can be found. A dance can tell the other bees about the quality of the food, and where to find it.

The waggle dance of a bee

The bee follows a figure-of-eight path, waggling its abdomen in the middle of the pattern.

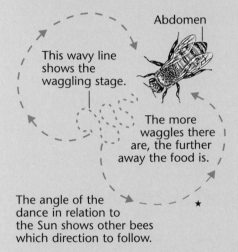

Abdomen

This wavy line shows the waggling stage.

The more waggles there are, the further away the food is.

The angle of the dance in relation to the Sun shows other bees which direction to follow.

MAKING NOISES

Most animals use sounds to communicate a wide variety of messages. Sounds can be produced using different parts of the body.

When you hear a bird sing, it may be trying to attract a mate, or warning other birds not to come near its territory. The bird sings using a part of its windpipe called the **syrinx**.

Position of syrinx ———

Some insects, such as locusts, make sounds by **stridulation**. The insect rubs together two body parts, usually the legs and wings, to make a shrill chirp or whine. The noise attracts females.

A grasshopper rubs tiny pegs on its legs against its wings to make a noise.

A female moth can release scent (pheromones) into the air.

A male moth can detect minute traces of the female's scent from over a mile away.

CHEMICAL MESSAGES

Many animals communicate by releasing chemicals called **pheromones** into the air. Some insects, for example, release incredibly powerful pheromones to attract a mate.

A number of male animals spray urine, or release other chemicals from glands on their bodies, to mark their territory. Other animals recognize these smelly areas as belonging to that male, and stay well away.

ORDER OF IMPORTANCE

Animals that live in groups are called **social** animals. In some social species, such as wolves, body language is used to show the importance of each animal.

Wolf at the top of the pack

Ears pricked up

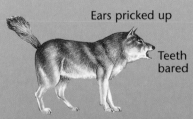

Teeth bared

Tail and body held straight

A more powerful wolf, called a **dominant** wolf, nips weaker wolves, called **subordinates**, on the neck. This shows that he is more important.

Wolf at the bottom of the pack

Ears flat against head

Crouched body

Tail tucked under body

See for yourself

You may sometimes see a pet dog roll onto its back, showing its vulnerable neck or belly. It does this to show you that it is a subordinate, and will not attack you.

Internet links

Go to **www.usborne-quicklinks.com** for links to the following Web sites:

Web site 1 Learn how caterpillars and butterflies protect themselves from predators.

Web site 2 Watch an animated bee dance.

Web site 3 Hear the messages sent by howling wolves.

Web site 4 A large archive of crocodile and alligator sounds, with explanations of their meaning.

Web site 5 Listen to many different animal sounds.

ANIMAL SENSES

Most bats have small eyes, but large, sensitive ears.

All animals need **senses**, that is, they must be able to take in information from around them and to respond. Sensitive cells called **receptors**, found on or just under the surface of an animal's body, collect this information and send messages to its brain. There, the messages are turned into **sensations**, such as sights and sounds.

HEARING

Most land animals hear by detecting air movements called **sound waves**. These hit a thin surface called the **tympanum**, which vibrates. Tiny bones pass the vibrations on inside, and messages are sent to the brain. In many animals, a channel, and often an outer body part, leads the sound waves into the body. In these cases, the whole thing is called an **ear**, and the tympanum is called the **eardrum**.

A mammal's ear ★

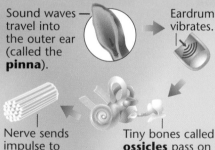

Sound waves travel into the outer ear (called the **pinna**).

Eardrum vibrates.

Nerve sends impulse to the brain.

Tiny bones called **ossicles** pass on vibrations.

See for yourself

Stretch some plastic film tightly across the top of a tube, such as a cardboard tube from inside a roll of kitchen paper, and put a few grains of rice on it. Ask someone to clap beneath the tube. See how the air vibrations move the film, which moves the rice. This is how sound waves move the eardrum and ossicles.

Some animals have a simpler structure, with the tympanum on the body surface, and a less complex system inside. This is then usually called a **tympanal organ**. In some animals, such as frogs, the tympanal organ is on the head, but others, such as crickets, have them on their legs.

Position of frog's tympanal organ

Echo location describes the way that some animals detect the size and position of objects around them. Bats, for example, give out very high-pitched sounds as they fly. The sound waves bounce off nearby objects, and return to the bat. These echoes help bats to avoid obstacles, and to find food in the dark.

Bat sends out high-pitched sounds (shown in blue).

Insect

★

Returning echo (shown in red)

BALANCE

In many species, the brain keeps the body balanced using information from sensitive cells in the ears along with messages from the eyes. Some creatures, though, have specialized body parts which help them to balance.

Jellyfish, for example, have sac-like organs of balance called **statocysts**. These contain tiny grains called **statoliths** which move around as the animal swims. The grains touch sensitive cells, which tell the animal which way up its body is.

Floating jellyfish

Flies have small, modified back wings called **haltères**. These are used to keep the animal's body balanced as it flies.

Haltère

SIGHT

Many animals have **eyes**. These are the organs which allow them to see their surroundings. Eyes contain sensors called **photoreceptors**, which detect light.

Insects and some other creatures, such as crabs, have **compound eyes**. Each eye is made up of hundreds of tiny lenses. Each lens sees an individual image. The animal's brain puts together this information to make a complete **mosaic image**.

Compound eye

Mosaic image of flower as seen by an ★ insect

Many animals' eyes have a slit in the middle called a **pupil**. This expands and contracts to let in different amounts of light. Animals which are active at night, called **nocturnal** animals, have large eyes, with pupils that can open very wide to let in as much light as possible.

Cat's eyes in bright light

Cat's eyes in dim light ★

Nocturnal animals and some deep-sea fish have a shiny layer at the back of their eyes called a **tapetum**. This acts like a mirror, collecting whatever light is available. When you see a cat's eyes shining in the dark, light is reflecting off its tapetum.

EYE POSITION

The area that an animal can see is called its **field of vision**. It depends on the position of the animal's eyes. Most plant-eating animals, for instance, have eyes on the sides of their head. This helps them to look out for predators while they are grazing. This kind of vision is called **lateral vision**.

This suslik can watch all around for predators.

Predators and tree-dwelling animals have eyes on the front of their head, which gives them **binocular vision**. This allows them to focus on objects in the distance, such as their prey.

Monkeys, apes and humans also have **stereoscopic vision**. Each eye views things from a slightly different angle. The brain joins the two views to form a 3D image.

The position of this orang-utan's eyes help it to judge distances when swinging from tree to tree.

See for yourself

You can do a simple test to show that humans have stereoscopic vision. Hold both hands at arm's length, with the index fingers extended and pointing towards each other. Close one eye and try to bring your two fingertips together. You will find this is harder to do without both eyes open.

Internet links

Go to **www.usborne-quicklinks.com** for links to the following Web sites:

Web site 1 Discover different animals' "Super Senses".

Web site 2 See patterns, human faces and other creatures through the eyes of a honey bee.

Web site 3 Find out about birds' senses.

Web site 4 Learn more about how bats use echo location.

Web site 5 Fascinating facts about animal senses.

TOUCH

The sense of touch can help an animal to find its way around, or to bond with other members of its species. For example, some animals groom each other, or rub their body parts together.

Sensors called **tactile receptors** allow an animal to detect touch. Animals with backbones, called **vertebrates**, usually have tactile receptors covering most of their bodies. Animals without backbones, called **invertebrates**, only have them on particular parts.

TENTACLES

Tentacles are long, flexible structures found in many molluscs, such as snails, and some sea creatures. In most cases, the animal uses its tentacles to grasp food and feel its way around.

An octopus has eight sensitive tentacles.

WHISKERS

Most mammals, such as cats and mice, have long, stiff hairs, called **whiskers** or **vibrissae**, on their faces. These are very sensitive to touch.

Nerve endings at the base of this hamster's whiskers can detect the slightest movement.

ANTENNAE

Many animals, such as insects and crustaceans (crabs and related creatures), have whip-like, jointed structures called **antennae** or **feelers** on their heads.

Antennae help an animal identify smells and tastes. They can detect changes in air currents, and the texture of a surface. Some animals, such as barnacles, use antennae to attach themselves to something. Others may use them for swimming.

SENSITIVE BRISTLES

The hard body covering of most invertebrates, such as insects, is not very sensitive. For this reason, many invertebrates have bristles called **setae** which stick out of their bodies. At the base of each seta is a nerve which responds to vibrations or air movement.

A longhorn beetle's large antennae are jointed and very flexible.

This beetle's body has a covering of tiny, sensitive hairs (setae).

SMELL AND TASTE

Organs used for smelling and tasting contain sensors called **chemoreceptors**. These are usually in an animal's mouth, but can also be found on other parts of the body.

Some fish, for example, have taste and smell sensors all over their bodies. Many insects, though, have chemoreceptors only in certain places, such as on the ends of their legs. These allow the insects to taste their food simply by walking on it.

Sensors on the feet of this fly let it taste the substance it is walking over and help it to decide whether or not to eat it.

Many arthropods* also have feeler-like organs, called **palps**, formed from their mouthparts. Palps contain chemoreceptors which allow the animal to smell and taste. Some touch-sensitive organs are also called palps.

See for yourself

The senses of smell and taste often work together. This is why you may find it hard to taste food when you have a cold and your nose is blocked. Try pinching your nose while eating something, and see how well your sense of taste works.

A snake brings scents and tastes into its mouth by flicking its tongue out and in. Two pits called **Jacobson's organs** in the roof of its mouth can identify these scents and tastes. This helps the snake to track prey. In addition, some snakes have a **pit organ** on their head, which can detect their prey's body heat from a distance.

OTHER SENSES

Fish and some amphibians* have two tube-like channels in their bodies called **lateral lines**. These lie along the sides of the body, just under the skin, and are filled with water. Lateral lines detect currents and pressure changes in the water caused by other animals.

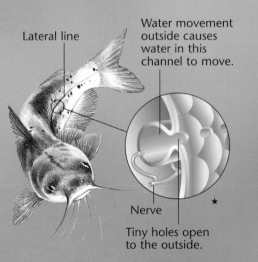

Lateral line

Water movement outside causes water in this channel to move.

Nerve

Tiny holes open to the outside.

A shark can detect electrical pulses given off by creatures nearby. It does this using small chambers called **ampullae of Lorenzi** in its head. Sensitive hairs in these chambers connect to nerve cells which detect electricity. This sense is called **electroreception**.

Coral snake flicking its tongue out and in to taste the air

Scientists are not certain what senses help a bird to migrate*, but they have many theories. It is possible that birds can sense the Earth's magnetic field and use it as a guide.

Arctic terns use many senses to find their way to the Antarctic and back.

Internet links

Go to **www.usborne-quicklinks.com** for links to the following Web sites:

Web site 1 Lots of detailed information about insects' antennae, eyes, hearing and other senses.

Web site 2 Read about the various senses of butterflies and moths, and how they are used.

Web site 3 Find out about the amazing sense of magnetic detection used by different animals.

Web site 4 A detailed and interesting look at all of a bird's senses.

Amphibians, 25, 52; Arthropods, 52; Migration, 39.

CREATING NEW LIFE

Every living thing can create more of its own kind. This process is called **reproduction**. Most animals pair up to do this, in couples made up of one male and one female partner. Simple creatures, though, can **clone**, or copy, their own bodies, without needing a partner. This is called **asexual reproduction**.

This Paramecium is beginning to split into two halves. Each one will become a new individual.

SPLITTING

Single-celled creatures, such as amoebas, reproduce asexually by dividing into identical halves. This is called **binary fission**.

Some tiny organisms reproduce many times by constantly splitting. This is called **multiple fission**. In this way, large numbers of new individuals, called **daughter cells**, are produced in a short time.

A few creatures, such as corals, remain joined to their parent after asexual reproduction has taken place. This is known as **incomplete fission**.

This coral reef is built up of many individual corals joined together.

BUDDING

Some simple animals, such as hydra, reproduce by forming growths or **buds** from their bodies. This is called **budding**. Each bud eventually breaks off and becomes a new individual.

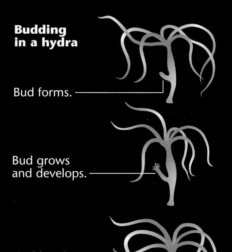

Budding in a hydra

Bud forms.

Bud grows and develops.

Bud breaks away.

BREAKING DOWN

A small number of animals can produce new individuals from parts of their bodies. This is called **fragmentation**.

Fragmentation in a flatworm

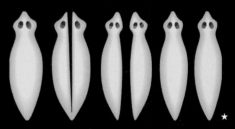

If a flatworm is split into pieces, each piece can become a new worm.

BUILDING UP

Some creatures, such as starfish, sea cucumbers and certain lizards, can re-grow parts of their body which have broken off. This is called **regeneration**.

Starfish

If an arm is broken off, a new one will grow to replace it.

MALE AND FEMALE

A result of asexual reproduction is that any weaknesses in the parent are always passed to the young. **Sexual reproduction***, by contrast, involves joining the sex cells of a male and a female. The young then inherit features, called **traits**, from both parents.

In most species, males and females are separate. However, some creatures, such as snails and earthworms, have both male and female sex cells in their bodies. These creatures are called **hermaphrodites**.

Snail with eggs

After fertilization has taken place (see below), a snail lays eggs which it buries in a hole.

The joining of male and female sex cells is called **fertilization**. Hermaphrodites generally do not fertilize themselves, but swap male sex cells to fertilize each other. The young inherit traits from both parents.

See for yourself

When two earthworms swap sex cells, a saddle-like body part called the **clitellum** makes a sticky substance which holds their bodies together. Next time you see a worm, look for its clitellum.

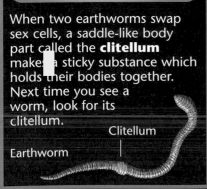

Clitellum

Earthworm

SEXUAL AND ASEXUAL

Tiny insects called aphids have a reproductive cycle which has both sexual and asexual stages.

During the warm spring and summer months, there is plenty of food to eat. The female aphids reproduce asexually. They produce many live female young, and later live male young. These all grow from the sex cells inside the females' bodies, without being fertilized by male sex cells. This is called **parthenogenesis**.

When the summer is over, the aphids reproduce sexually. After fertilization, the females lay eggs, from which new females hatch the following spring.

Aphids on a flower

During the spring and summer, the number of aphids increases rapidly.

In a colony of bees, only the queen produces young. She reproduces sexually, receiving sex cells from the males and laying fertilized eggs. These develop into females called **workers**. The queen also lays eggs that have not been fertilized. These develop into males called **drones**.

Drone (male)   Queen bee   Worker (female)

Internet links

Go to **www.usborne-quicklinks.com** for links to the following Web sites:

Web site 1 Examine a virtual worm and click on its clitellum to learn about reproduction.

Web site 2 A short page on reproduction in corals.

Web site 3 A brief and simple introduction to asexual reproduction in various animals.

Web site 4 A look at reproduction in hydra, with detailed microscope images.

SEXUAL REPRODUCTION

Most animals pair up or **mate** with another member of their species to produce young. A male and a female come together in a process called **sexual reproduction**. A single sex cell from the male fertilizes a sex cell from the female to create a new individual.

FINDING A PARTNER

Many animals use sound, scents called pheromones*, visual displays (see page 28) or other devices to attract a mate. Once together, the two may go through a **courtship ritual** of some kind before mating. Usually, the male displays to the female, trying to impress her. In some species, especially certain types of birds, the two may "dance", or perform, together.

In most species, the male leaves the female after mating, but some pairs stay together for many years, producing new young each year.

FERTILIZATION

Fertilization takes place when a male sex cell, called a **sperm**, joins with a female sex cell, called an **ovum**. Each ovum can only be fertilized by one sperm. This creates the first cell of a new organism. As it grows, it is called an **embryo**.

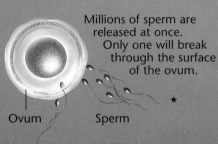

Millions of sperm are released at once. Only one will break through the surface of the ovum.

Ovum   Sperm   *

A female frog lays many soft eggs.

External fertilization takes place mostly in water-dwelling animals, such as fish and amphibians*. The female lays many eggs containing her ova, and then the male fertilizes them by covering them with sperm. The closer he is to the eggs, the more likely it is that his sperm will fertilize them. A male frog, for example, grasps the female's body and deposits sperm on the eggs as she lays them.

Internal fertilization takes place inside the female's body. Almost all land animals, such as mammals, are fertilized in this way. The male puts his sperm directly into the female's body, usually through a specialized organ called a **penis**.

A pair of swans will stay together for life.

* Amphibians, 25, 52; Pheromones, 29.

LAYING EGGS

Egg-laying animals are described as **oviparous**. Most reptiles, insects, birds and fish are oviparous. The eggs may be fertilized externally or they may result from internal fertilization. There are two main types of eggs.

Most fish and amphibians, such as the frog on the left, produce hundreds of tiny, soft eggs, called **spawn**. These often contain young which do not look like the adults at all.

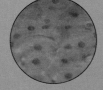

The tiny black dots in this frogspawn are the developing young.

Most land animals, such as birds and reptiles, produce a smaller number of **cleidoic eggs**. In these, the embryo is fed by a food store called a **yolk** and protected by a hard shell. When the eggs hatch, the young are usually miniature versions of the adults.

A cleidoic egg

The **albumen** provides the embryo with protein and water.

Twisted strands of albumen hold the yolk in place.

Yolk

Bird embryo

Oxygen in

Gases are exchanged through shell and air space.

Carbon dioxide out

GIVING BIRTH

Animals that give birth to live young are described as **viviparous**. Many animals of this kind are mammals. The baby grows inside the female in a sac called the **womb** or **uterus**. An organ called the **placenta** feeds the baby inside the womb. After a period of time, muscles in the female's body contract and the baby is pushed out.

The length of time a baby spends inside the womb is called the **gestation period**. It varies from species to species.

After giving birth, most mammals, such as this zebra, lick their young clean.

ANIMAL FAMILIES

Many baby animals are born helpless, and depend entirely on their mother to protect and feed them. A mammal feeds her young with milk from her **mammary glands**. The babies drink milk, or **suckle**, until they are old enough to eat solid food.

A gorilla gives birth to one baby every few years. The baby suckles until it is about three or four years old.

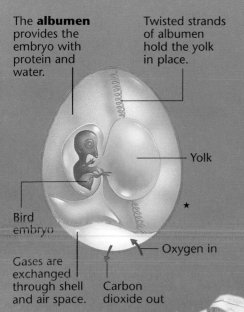

Almost all birds and some reptiles also feed and protect their young after they are born. In some species, both parents share these duties.

A female emperor penguin protects her chick while the male feeds at sea.

When the male returns, both parents take turns to feed and protect the chick.

See for yourself

In the springtime, look in ponds for clumps of frogspawn. Although there may seem to be lots of eggs, many of the young will be eaten by predators after they hatch. Very few will survive to become adult frogs.

Internet links

Go to **www.usborne-quicklinks.com** for links to the following Web sites:

Web site 1 "Parenthood" essay about nesting and egg-laying, from David Attenborough's TV series "The Life of Birds".

Web site 2 Read more about eggs.

Web site 3 Find out more about animals that give birth to live young.

Web site 4 Sounds and video clips of real baby animals.

Web site 5 Interesting information about reproduction in bears.

LIFE CYCLES

Many changes take place between the beginning and end of an animal's life: it grows, develops, and produces young. These patterns of growth and behaviour are called a **life cycle**. Some animal life cycles take many years to complete. Many insects, by contrast, complete their life cycle in a few months.

Life cycle of a locust (incomplete metamorphosis)

Female lays eggs, which hatch into nymphs.

Locust nymph, called a **hopper**

Hopper sheds its skin several times.

Locust is now fully grown.

METAMORPHOSIS

Some animals, such as insects and frogs, change their form completely in the course of their life cycle. This is called **metamorphosis**. There are two kinds of metamorphosis: complete and incomplete. In **complete metamorphosis**, the young form looks very different from the adult form.

Insects such as butterflies, moths and ladybirds undergo complete metamorphosis. Their young, called **larvae**, feed and grow, then develop hard cases called **pupae**. Inside the pupae, they change into adults.

Life cycle of a butterfly

Eggs

Larva, called **caterpillar**

Pupa

Adult emerges from pupa.

Other insects, such as the locust above, go through **incomplete metamorphosis**. This means that the young, called **nymphs**, look similar to their parents, although some body parts, such as their wings, are not yet formed. Nymphs shed their skins several times as they become larger. As they grow, their wings and reproductive organs develop.

The adult form of an insect that has gone through either complete or incomplete metamorphosis is known as the **imago**.

Life cycle of a frog (complete metamorphosis)

Female lays eggs called **spawn** in water.

Eggs hatch into **tadpoles**.

Back legs and lungs develop.

Front legs grow, tail will disappear.

Young frog leaves water and grows to full size.

Complete metamorphosis often provides a form in which the animal can survive the winter. The young usually live in different habitats and have different diets from the adults, so they do not compete for food or space.

See for yourself

If you are able to find any frogspawn in a pond during the springtime, go back and look at the tadpoles every week after they hatch. After about eight weeks, you will notice their tiny legs starting to develop.

Migrating wildebeest crossing a river

These Canada geese, like almost all geese, migrate to their breeding grounds every year.

MAKING A JOURNEY

At some stage in their life cycles, many animals travel long distances in large groups, often to breed or find food. This journey is called **migration**.

Many birds migrate twice every year (to their breeding or feeding grounds and back). They use the position of the Sun, stars and features of the land to find their way. Many land animals, such as wildebeest, move with the seasons to find food. They may have to overcome obstacles, such as rivers.

MIGRATION IN WATER

Some animals, such as salmon and eels, may only migrate once in their lifetime. The journey is long and hard, and few fish survive to breed again.

Life cycle of a salmon

Salmon travel upstream to breed. They swim from the sea to the rivers where they were hatched.

When they arrive, the females lay eggs in the riverbed, in hollows dug out with their tails.

The young salmon, called **fry**, live in the rivers for about three years before swimming to the sea, where they remain until ready to breed.

A LONG REST

Many animals which do not migrate survive seasons of cold or drought in a sleep-like state called **dormancy**. Dormancy during a drought is called **aestivation**. Dormancy in winter is called **hibernation**.

Before hibernating, animals collect food. Some eat it all and develop a layer of body fat to keep them alive through the winter. Others store the food and wake occasionally to eat.

Hibernating animals, such as this dormouse, settle down in a safe, well-hidden place.

The animal's breathing and heartbeat slow down, and its body temperature drops. It becomes active again in the spring, when food is available.

Internet links

Go to **www.usborne-quicklinks.com** for links to the following Web sites:

Web site 1 Visit the London Butterfly House for an animated description of the life cycle of a butterfly.

Web site 2 Read an illustrated description of frog mating and metamorphosis.

Web site 3 Information on monarch butterfly metamorphosis and migration patterns.

Web site 4 Track the migration of whales, eagles and other animals.

Web site 5 The life cycle of a salmon, with photographs.

ECOLOGY

The world can be divided into different areas, each with its own plants and animals. All living things are suited to their surroundings, or **environment**, and they depend on each other for survival. The study of the relationships between plants, animals and their environment is called **ecology**.

ANIMAL HOMES

The natural home of an animal or group of animals is called its **habitat**. The plants and animals that live together in a particular habitat are called a **community**. A community, together with non-living parts of the environment such as air and water, form an **ecosystem**. Smaller ecosystems can be found within a larger one, for example a rotting log in a forest.

A single rainforest flower may be a habitat for frogs and many insects.

Frog

See for yourself

Lift up a stone and see what lives in the habitat beneath it. You will probably find creatures which like damp, dark places, such as slugs, earthworms and woodlice. Remember to leave everything as you found it.

SUCCESSION

Sometimes a habitat and its community are destroyed – for example in a forest fire. After the fire, different plants and animals replace each other as the habitat develops. This process is called **ecological succession**. Eventually, a community is established that will remain unchanged, as long as its environment is stable. This is called a **climax community**.

Succession in a disused field

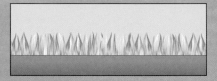

First or **pioneer community** is made up of grasses. This becomes a home for insects and small mammals.

Shrubs and bushes begin to grow. Mammals such as rabbits join the community.

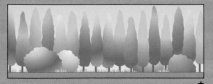

Climax community of trees can support a wide variety of animals, including foxes and badgers.

FOOD FOR ALL

The role of an animal in its community, including what it eats and where it lives, is called its **ecological niche**. Two species cannot live in the same niche at the same time. If they tried, one would die out or be driven away.

All of the animals below can survive together in the African grasslands, because their diets are slightly different, so they occupy different niches.

Grassland ecological niches

Giraffes reach up to feed on the top parts of trees.

Elephants stretch their trunks to browse on twigs, leaves and branches.

Gerenuks stand on their back legs to pluck leaves from bushes.

Rhinos eat leaves in the middle of bushes.

BIOMES

Biomes are the largest ecosystems into which the Earth's surface can be divided. Most are named after the main types of vegetation they contain. Each biome has its own unique combination of vegetation and wildlife. Below, you can see a type of animal that is normally found in each major biome.

Map showing main world biomes

Europe

Asia

North America

South America

Africa

Australasia

Antarctica

Tundra areas are very cold and windy. Few plants or animals can survive there.

Snowshoe hare

Tropical rainforests are hot and wet all year, and are rich in plant and animal life.

Morpho butterfly

Scrublands (called **maquis**) have hot, dry winds in the summer.

Chameleon

Coniferous forests contain evergreen trees and are cool all year round.

Black bear

Deserts are hot and dry and contain few living things.

Scorpion

Oceans contain a huge number of ecosystems and cover most of the surface of the Earth.

Ocean goldfish

Tropical grasslands are mostly made up of grasses and trees.

Lion

Temperate grasslands are open, grassy plains with few trees.

Prairie dog

Polar areas are covered in ice and snow. Few living things can survive there.

Walrus

Red squirrel

Deciduous forest areas have warm summers and cold winters.

Mountains are mostly cold and bare at the top, with vegetation at the foot.

Bighorn sheep

Polar bears can live in the Arctic because their thick skin and shaggy coat protect them from the cold.

Internet links

Go to **www.usborne-quicklinks.com** for links to the following Web sites:

Web site 1 Take a tour of a rainforest in Costa Rica.

Web site 2 An exploration of marine ecosystems.

Web site 3 An exploration of freshwater ecosystems.

Web site 4 An introduction to ecology and biomes.

Web site 5 Explore the Serengeti National Park and learn about some of the different habitats found there.

Web site 6 Useful information about ecosystems, biomes and habitats, with activities.

FOOD AND ENERGY

Plants make their own food using water, carbon dioxide from the air and energy from the Sun. They are described as **autotrophic**. Animals, though, depend on other living things for food and are described as **heterotrophic**. Animals get energy by eating plants or other animals that have themselves eaten plants.

This dragonfly gets its energy by eating plant-eating insects.

FOOD CHAINS

All animals are part of a **food chain**. This is a series of living things, each of which is eaten by the next in line. The position of a living thing within a food chain is its **trophic level**, with plants at the first level. Plants are called **producers**, because they make food which provides energy. Animals in a food chain are called **consumers**.

Within a food chain, a herbivore (plant-eating animal) is known as a **primary** or **first order consumer**. An animal that eats a primary consumer is called a **secondary consumer**, and so on. Many carnivores (meat eaters) eat both herbivores and smaller carnivores. They are therefore secondary consumers on some occasions and tertiary consumers on others.

Food chains also contain tiny organisms called **decomposers**. These include bacteria, fungi and many invertebrates. Decomposers break down dead plant and animal matter, and return minerals from them to the soil.

A woodland food chain

Fourth trophic level (T4)

Tertiary consumer

Hawk

Third trophic level (T3)

Secondary consumer

Thrush

Second trophic level (T2)

Primary consumer

Snail

First trophic level (T1)

Producer

Buttercups

Fungi release chemicals that break down plant and animal matter into simpler substances.

ENERGY TRANSFER

Most of the food an animal eats is used up by its body, and some is stored. When that animal is eaten, the next consumer only gains the stored energy. Therefore, much less energy is available at the next stage in the chain.

Alligators eat animals from every level of their food chain to get the energy they need.

Each trophic level has far fewer consumers in it than the level below. This is because the animals have to eat more food to get the energy they need. This can be shown as a **pyramid of numbers**.

Pyramid of numbers

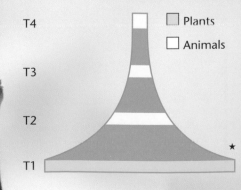

T4

T3

T2

T1

☐ Plants
☐ Animals

BIOMASS

Biomass is the combined weight of all living things in a habitat. The biomass of plants is much higher than that of any other living things in the same area. At each level of a food chain, there are fewer living things than in the level below, with a lower combined biomass.

This can be shown in a diagram called a **pyramid of biomass**.

Pyramid of biomass

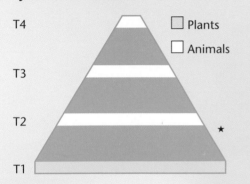

- ☐ Plants
- ☐ Animals

T4
T3
T2
T1

A meadow is an example of a habitat, and its biomass could be shown by a pyramid like the one above. The total biomass of plants at T1 in a meadow can be several thousand kilograms. Several hundred kilograms of insects at T2 may live on these plants.

The small mammals at T3, which eat the plants and insects, have a combined biomass of about 150kg. A single fox at T4, which feeds on the small animals, has a biomass of around 5kg.

See for yourself

Next time you eat, think about what trophic level you occupy. For instance, if you are eating vegetables, you are on the second trophic level. If you are eating meat, you are on a higher trophic level.

FOOD WEBS

A series of interlinked food chains is called a **food web**. Many food chains are linked because very few animals feed on just one thing. For example, most carnivores eat whatever small animals they can find. A herbivore might eat different types of plants depending on the season.

Interdependence describes a number of living things relying on each other and the environment to stay alive, for example in a food web.

A rainforest food web

Jaguar

Peccary

Capybara

Tamandua

Agouti

White-faced capuchin

Grubs

Insects

Water plants

Leaves

Fruit

Food webs are easily damaged by humans. For instance, in 1910, wardens in the Grand Canyon Game Reserve tried to protect the deer population by shooting the animals that ate them. The numbers of deer increased, but there was not enough food for them all. Eventually, many starved to death.

Numbers of plant eaters, like these deer, can become too high without meat eaters to control them.

Internet links

Go to **www.usborne-quicklinks.com** for links to the following Web sites:

Web site 1 A simple introduction to food chains.

Web site 2 Find out more about biomass and its uses.

Web site 3 A detailed description of food chains.

Web site 4 An interesting experiment showing the cycle of energy in an ecosystem.

Web site 5 Discover who eats what in a stream.

BALANCE IN NATURE

Animals and plants depend on each other, and on the **abiotic** (non-living) parts of the environment, to stay alive. Essential substances, such as carbon, nitrogen and water, constantly move through plants and animals, as well as through the land, sea and air. These circulations are called **cycles**. Many human activities, such as fuel burning, affect the delicate balance between living things and their environment, putting their lives in danger.

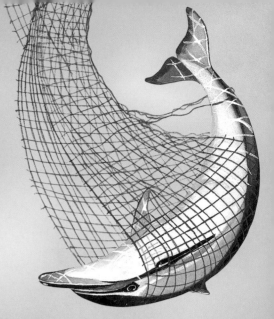

Many dolphins and other sea creatures are killed accidentally in commercial fishing nets.

THE NITROGEN CYCLE

The gas **nitrogen** is constantly recycled through the living world. Plants and animals need nitrogen-based substances to build chemicals called **proteins** in their bodies. Plants absorb nitrogen in the form of **nitrates** from the soil and use it to grow. Animals get nitrogen by eating plants, or plant-eating animals.

When living things die, bacteria and fungi break them down and nitrogen is released back into the soil in a chemical called **ammonia**. Other bacteria change this into nitrates, which are taken up by new plants.

These dung beetles bury balls of dung. Bacteria in the soil release nitrogen from the dung as they break it down.

THE CARBON CYCLE

Different forms of **carbon** are recycled through the living world. For instance, plants take in carbon dioxide from the air and use it, along with water and sunlight, to make food. Animals eat plants, and their bodies break down the plant matter and use the carbon for growth and energy.

Plant eaters such as cows take in carbon from plants. Meat eaters gain carbon by eating plant eaters.

Chemical reactions inside animals and plants turn food into energy, and carbon dioxide is produced as waste. Animals release carbon dioxide into the air as they breathe out, and plants give it off at night when they are not making food. Carbon dioxide is also released back into the air when dead plant and animal matter breaks down.

THE WATER CYCLE

The water that falls as rain drains into rivers, then into the sea. It evaporates, rises, then forms tiny droplets of moisture in the air. These form clouds and fall again as rain. In this way, water is constantly recycled between the air and the earth.

The water cycle

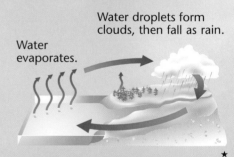

Water droplets form clouds, then fall as rain.

Water evaporates.

Plants and animals also release water. For example, animals do this when they breathe out.

See for yourself

You can see water in the air you breathe out by breathing heavily on a mirror. The warm moisture in your breath cools as it touches the mirror's surface, and turns into tiny drops of water.

POLLUTION

Pollution is damage usually caused to the environment by human activities, such as garbage dumping. Waste chemicals from factories are pumped into rivers and seas, and fumes from burning fuels and vehicle exhausts pollute the air. Animals that live in a seriously polluted environment may become unable to breed, or fall sick and die.

This seabird is trapped on a seashore polluted with oil from a damaged oil tanker. This type of pollution can wipe out the sea life in an area.

DEADLY CHEMICALS

When dangerous chemicals are released into the environment, food chains* are often damaged. For example, **insecticides** are poisons used to kill insects that harm crops. These poisons are often taken in by other small creatures. When predators eat these animals, they also take in the poison, and so it is passed to animals at higher levels in the food chain.

This happened on a large scale in the 1950s and 1960s, when an insecticide called DDT was widely used. It entered some food chains, becoming more concentrated at each level. Eventually, it killed thousands of birds of prey at the top of these chains.

THREATENED SEA LIFE

Many species of fish and shellfish are becoming endangered* because too many have been caught to provide food for people. This is called **overfishing**. The remaining fish cannot produce enough young to replace the ones that have been caught.

Some fishermen are now using nets with larger holes. These allow young fish to escape and breed, so their numbers do not decrease too much.

Young fish can escape from a net with large holes.

This farmer is spraying his crops with insecticides. The insecticides kill pests, but they may also harm many useful creatures that live in the same place.

Internet links

Go to **www.usborne-quicklinks.com** for links to the following Web sites:

Web site 1 Learn about the role of worms as recyclers.

Web site 2 Watch a movie about the water cycle.

Web site 3 A simple summary of the natural cycles.

Web site 4 A colourful, eco-friendly site with games, activities and facts.

Web site 5 An advanced description of the water cycle.

Web site 6 A fun Web site about the environment.

* Endangered species, 46; Food chains, 42.

CONSERVATION

Many animal species are in danger of dying out completely. This is known as becoming **extinct**. Some animals are hunted for useful body parts, such as fur, but most are threatened by loss of habitat. Nature **conservation** aims to protect animals and look after the Earth's natural resources to ensure the future of all living things.

Koalas were once faced with extinction, but conservation efforts have been successful and their numbers are increasing.

DISAPPEARING SPECIES

Since life on Earth began, many species have disappeared as a result of natural changes in the environment. This is called the **background rate of extinction**. More recently, human activity has led to a huge increase in the extinction rate. However, people are now taking action to protect disappearing species.

Tiger hunting has been banned since 1970, but tigers are still illegally killed by poachers.

An animal that is in danger of becoming extinct in the wild is described as an **endangered species**. If a species is likely to become endangered in the near future, it is described as **threatened**. In many countries, it is now illegal to kill, capture or sell animals which are threatened or endangered.

GUARDING ANIMALS

Although many laws have been passed to protect animals, it is hard to make people obey them. For instance, it is illegal to hunt elephants and rhinos, but poachers still kill them for their tusks and horns. In Africa, many rhinos and elephants are now kept under close guard.

This rhino has had its horns removed. In parts of Africa, people are trying to save rhinos by removing their horns, so poachers will have no reason to kill them.

NATURE RESERVES

To preserve the world's threatened wildlife, areas have been set aside as **nature reserves**, where plants and animals can live in safety.

Wherever possible, tourists are allowed to visit these reserves. With the proper control, tourism is harmless to wildlife, and can be an excellent source of money for poorer countries.

Kenya earns millions of dollars every year from tourists who come to see elephants in nature reserves.

SAVING HABITATS

Major ecosystems*, such as coral reefs and rainforests, play a vital role in supporting life on Earth. Coral reefs are home to huge numbers of living things, which recycle oxygen and minerals through the oceans. Many countries are trying to protect their reefs. For instance, Australia has a 2,250km stretch of protected coral reefs called the Great Barrier Reef Marine Park.

Many thousands of plant and animal species live in or around coral reefs. When a reef is damaged or destroyed, all these living things are affected.

Rainforests are vital to all life because they recycle large amounts of carbon and nitrogen, which plants and animals need to survive. Vast areas of rainforest have already been destroyed, but people are working together to preserve the areas that remain.

Over half of all plant and animal species on Earth live in rainforests. Without conservation efforts, many may die out.

CAPTIVE BREEDING

Sometimes, a species becomes so rare that it will certainly die out without human help. In such cases, scientists try to increase the animals' numbers by breeding them in captivity, such as in a reserve or a zoo. These animals are sometimes returned to the wild, but many lack the skills that they need to survive.

Golden lion tamarins are rare, but they breed successfully in captivity.

Some species are **slow breeders**, which means that they produce very few young at long intervals. Giant pandas, which are highly endangered, are slow breeders. A few have been born in captivity, but the panda's best chance for survival is to save its native bamboo forests from future harm.

Giant pandas cannot survive without a good supply of bamboo, as it makes up around 99% of their diet.

DANGER AREAS

The main threat to animals is loss of habitat, but they are also killed by pollution and hunting. Many species are also **endemic**. This means that they are found in only one place. Scientists can identify areas, called **hotspots**, which contain large numbers of an endemic species, and ensure that they are well protected.

Many birds, particularly parrots and macaws, are put in danger by the pet trade. Some are also killed for their striking feathers. Combined with habitat loss, this has led to a third of all parrot species becoming endangered in the wild. It is possible, though, that numbers can be increased through captive breeding.

Hyacinth macaws are highly valued as pets because of their striking appearance. They are now one of the rarest types of macaw.

Internet links

Go to **www.usborne-quicklinks.com** for links to the following Web sites:

Web site 1 A good starting point for learning about endangered species and action groups.

Web site 2 An excellent source of information on conservation and related issues.

Web site 3 A conservation Web site just for kids, with animal facts, wildlife news and games.

Web site 4 The official Web site of the World Wide Fund for Nature.

Web site 5 Lots of interesting facts about coral reefs, including information about the threats they face.

* Ecosystem, 40.

EVOLUTION

Most scientists believe that life on Earth started with very simple creatures and developed gradually, through a long series of changes. This idea is called the **theory of evolution**. By studying existing organisms and prehistoric remains, scientists try to explain how and why living things have changed over time.

Fossils such as this ammonite shell allow scientists to learn more about ancient life.

EVOLUTION

According to most scientists, the first tiny organisms on Earth were bacteria*, which first existed around 3,500 million years ago. They suggest that, over the course of many millions of years, living things developed to become the first animals, as shown here.

Evolution of main animal groups

500 million years ago
First fish evolved, with thick skin and no jaws. About 150 million years later, bony fish and cartilaginous fish* evolved.

Sacabambaspis

410 million years ago
First wingless insects appeared. About 110 million years later, winged insects evolved.

Meganeura

350 million years ago
Some water-dwelling creatures began to breathe air, and became the first amphibians*.

Ichthyostega

300 million years ago
First reptiles appeared. Dinosaurs evolved around 200 million years ago, and lived for 135 million years, before they rapidly died out.

Dimetrodon

200 million years ago
First small mammals appeared. After the dinosaurs died out, larger mammals started to evolve.

Megazostrodon

150 million years ago
First birds evolved from small species of dinosaurs.

Archaeopteryx

FOSSILS

When a plant or animal dies, its body rots away, but hard parts, such as the skeleton, may be preserved in sand and mud. Over millions of years, the sand and mud build up in layers, and eventually turn to rock with the preserved remains of the plant or animal, called a **fossil**, inside.

How a fossil forms ★

The animal's flesh rots away.

Layers of sand and mud cover the skeleton, and turn into rock with the shape of the skeleton inside.

See for yourself

Museums can often provide interesting information about fossils and dinosaurs. You could visit a local museum and find out if it has a fossil collection, or a dinosaur exhibit.

* Amphibians, 25, 52; Bacteria, 51; Cartilaginous fish, 11.

MASS EXTINCTION

Many scientists suggest that there have been five events in the Earth's history during which huge numbers of living things died at once. They call such an event a **mass extinction**. This normally happens as a result of sudden, dramatic changes in the Earth's climate. Many organisms cannot adapt to these changes, and so they die out.

Dinosaurs may have been killed off by a change in climate caused by a meteorite hitting the Earth.

Large reptiles, such as this Deinonychus, have not lived on the Earth for over 65 million years.

NATURAL SELECTION

In the 1850s, a British scientist, Charles Darwin, put forward the **theory of natural selection** to explain how evolution takes place. He suggested that individual organisms with qualities that help them to survive in their environment tend to live longer and pass on these useful qualities to their offspring.

In this way, over a very long period of time, most of the members of a species will have the useful qualities and be well suited to their environment.

Features which offer protection increase an animal's chances of survival, and are therefore more likely to be passed on from one generation to the next. This is known as **protective adaptation**.

An example of this is when patterns on an animal's body allow it to remain hidden from enemies. This is called **camouflage**.

Peppered moth (dark variety)

A type of moth, called the peppered moth, is often used to show how natural selection takes place. During the nineteenth century, many trees upon which peppered moths rested became blackened by soot from factories.

Both dark and pale peppered moths resting on a soot-covered tree trunk

Moths with pale wings were seen and eaten by birds, but the rare moths with dark wings survived, bred and increased in numbers. Now, however, there is less pollution from soot and the moths with pale wings are increasing again.

Peppered moth (pale variety)

Internet links

Go to **www.usborne-quicklinks.com** for links to the following Web sites:

Web site 1 A valuable source of information about dinosaur species, evolution and extinction.

Web site 2 The official Web site of the BBC series "Walking with Dinosaurs", with facts, games and more.

Web site 3 A detailed timeline, explaining how the Earth is thought to have developed.

Web site 4 Find out which prehistoric animals evolved or died out.

Web site 5 Read all about the evolution of the horse.

CLASSIFICATION

To make living things easier to study, biologists organize them into groups with similar features. Fitting organisms into groups that can be divided to form smaller groups is called **classification**. For example, an elephant and a mouse both belong to the mammal group, because they have hair and produce milk for their young. Within the mammal group, though, they belong to different sub-groups.

A mouse and an elephant look different, but they both belong to the mammal group.

BIOLOGICAL KEYS

Scientists classify an organism by identifying its main features and deciding how these are different from those of a similar species. The method used is called a **biological key**. A typical biological key is arranged in branches, as in the example below. At each branch the scientist asks "Does the specimen have...?" and there is a choice between two or more features. Each response leads to another set of options until the organism is identified.

Branching key

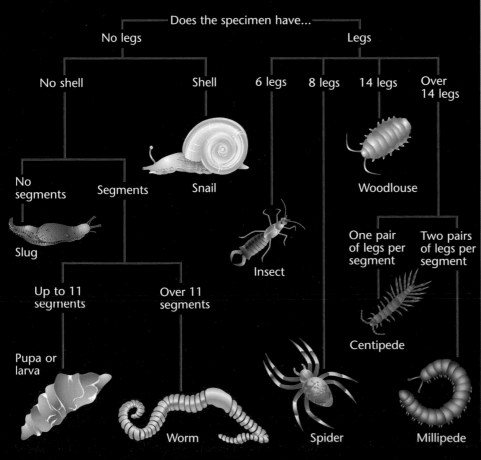

Does the specimen have...

- No legs
  - No shell
    - No segments — Slug
    - Segments
      - Up to 11 segments — Pupa or larva
      - Over 11 segments — Worm
  - Shell — Snail
- Legs
  - 6 legs — Insect
  - 8 legs — Spider
  - 14 legs — Woodlouse
  - Over 14 legs
    - One pair of legs per segment — Centipede
    - Two pairs of legs per segment — Millipede

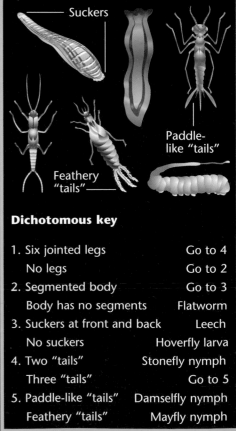

See for yourself

A key where you are given a choice of only two statements is called a **dichotomous key**. Try identifying the six creatures below using the key at the bottom of this box.

Look at each creature in turn and go through the dichotomous key, choosing one statement from each pair and following the instructions.

Suckers

Paddle-like "tails"

Feathery "tails"

Dichotomous key

1. Six jointed legs	Go to 4
No legs	Go to 2
2. Segmented body	Go to 3
Body has no segments	Flatworm
3. Suckers at front and back	Leech
No suckers	Hoverfly larva
4. Two "tails"	Stonefly nymph
Three "tails"	Go to 5
5. Paddle-like "tails"	Damselfly nymph
Feathery "tails"	Mayfly nymph

THE FIVE KINGDOMS

The largest groups into which living things can be sorted are called **kingdoms**.

Scientists currently divide living things into five main kingdoms: plants, fungi, animals, protista and monera. This method of classifying organisms is called **classical taxonomy**.

Viruses are not included in classical taxonomy. Although they can grow and reproduce, they are only able to exist within the cells of living things.

The five kingdoms of living things

Plants

Organisms such as trees, grass and flowers, that make their own food using sunlight.

Rosy periwinkle

Fungi

Organisms that are plant-like, but cannot make their own food. Instead, they mostly feed on dead plants and animals. Yeast and toadstools are examples of fungi.

Fly agaric

* Nucleus, 8.

Animals

Creatures that have more than one cell, can usually move around, and eat plants or other animals for food. Fish and birds are examples of animals.

Corkwing wrasse

Protista

Single-celled organisms, such as euglena, which share features with both plants and animals.

Euglena

Monera

Microscopic organisms, such as bacteria, which do not have nuclei* in their cells.

Salmonella bacterium (magnified many thousand times)

DIVIDING KINGDOMS

- Each kingdom can be broken down into levels called **taxonomic ranks** or **taxa**. The first rank is called a **phylum**. Each phylum breaks down into groups called **classes**. Classes are divided into **orders**, then **families**, then **genera**.

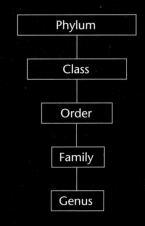

```
Phylum
  │
Class
  │
Order
  │
Family
  │
Genus
```

Each genus contains a number of **species**, which are individual groups of animals that are similar enough to breed together. Over the page, you can see how a single species can be traced from a phylum. In some cases, there are also mid-way groups, such as **sub-kingdoms** and **sub-phyla**.

Some phyla cannot be broken down in this way, because they have too few members. The next group after the phylum may therefore be an order, family, genus or even a species.

Internet links

Go to **www.usborne-quicklinks.com** for links to the following Web sites:

Web site 1 A fun introduction to the five kingdoms, with a movie and quiz.

Web site 2 Learn about any animal by typing its name into this site's own search engine.

Web site 3 A friendly look at the five kingdoms of living things.

THE ANIMAL KINGDOM

The animal kingdom contains a number of phyla, the main eight of which are shown below.
These can be sorted further into classes, orders, families, genera and species (see previous page).
Below, you can see how a single species, such as a timber wolf, can be traced from one of the
phyla. Each step down becomes more specific and includes fewer animals than the one before.

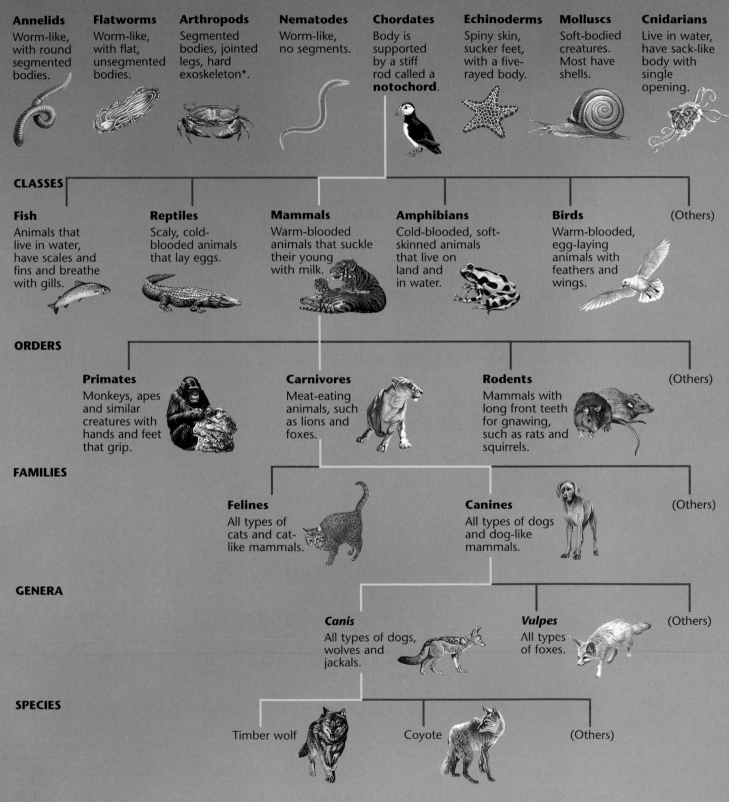

PHYLA

Annelids
Worm-like, with round segmented bodies.

Flatworms
Worm-like, with flat, unsegmented bodies.

Arthropods
Segmented bodies, jointed legs, hard exoskeleton*.

Nematodes
Worm-like, no segments.

Chordates
Body is supported by a stiff rod called a **notochord**.

Echinoderms
Spiny skin, sucker feet, with a five-rayed body.

Molluscs
Soft-bodied creatures. Most have shells.

Cnidarians
Live in water, have sack-like body with single opening.

CLASSES

Fish
Animals that live in water, have scales and fins and breathe with gills.

Reptiles
Scaly, cold-blooded animals that lay eggs.

Mammals
Warm-blooded animals that suckle their young with milk.

Amphibians
Cold-blooded, soft-skinned animals that live on land and in water.

Birds
Warm-blooded, egg-laying animals with feathers and wings.

(Others)

ORDERS

Primates
Monkeys, apes and similar creatures with hands and feet that grip.

Carnivores
Meat-eating animals, such as lions and foxes.

Rodents
Mammals with long front teeth for gnawing, such as rats and squirrels.

(Others)

FAMILIES

Felines
All types of cats and cat-like mammals.

Canines
All types of dogs and dog-like mammals.

(Others)

GENERA

Canis
All types of dogs, wolves and jackals.

Vulpes
All types of foxes.

(Others)

SPECIES

Timber wolf

Coyote

(Others)

NAMING THINGS

Living things are generally given one or more common names and a biological name. The **common name** is the one used by most people, such as tawny owl or red squirrel. A **biological name** is needed because an animal may have many common names, each one used in a different area. Biological names are usually in Latin. These names can be recognized by scientists all over the world.

These butterflies are so rare that they do not have common names, only biological names.

Callicore cyllene

Agrias claudina

Callicore mengeli

The biological name is created using the **binomial system**, which means that it is made up of two parts. The first part, called the **generic name**, is based on the organism's genus. The second part, called the **specific epithet**, identifies its species.

In many cases, a biological name refers to the animal's appearance, habitat or body features. For instance, a giraffe's biological name is *Giraffa camelopardalis*. *Giraffa* means "swift walker", *camel* means "camel-like", and *pardalis* means "marked like a leopard". So a giraffe is a swift-moving, camel-like animal with a patterned coat like a leopard.

SUB-SPECIES

In some cases, there are also **sub-species**, which have a third part added to their biological name. This can refer to the area in which the sub-species is found, or to a particular characteristic.

This tiger's name is *Panthera tigris sumatrae*. The third part of its name shows that it is a sub-species from Sumatra.

An animal's biological name often refers to a particular physical feature. For instance, *Giraffa* is based on an Arabic word meaning "swift walker".

INFORMAL GROUPS

Different species which share certain types of lifestyle can also be put together in informal groups, by using terms which describe this lifestyle. Social* and nocturnal* animals are two such terms, and there are other examples below.

An animal or plant which lives and feeds on another organism (called the **host**) is known as a **parasite**. Some parasites are harmful to their hosts.

Fleas are common parasites which feed on the blood of their host.

Mutualists are animals or plants which live close together in a situation where both gain. For example, birds called oxpeckers eat parasites that live on the hides of larger animals, such as buffalo and zebra. The larger animals benefit in turn from having the pests removed.

Two species in a relationship where one gains without affecting the other are called **commensals**. House mice, for example, live where humans are found, and feed on their scraps.

Internet links

Go to **www.usborne-quicklinks.com** for links to the following Web sites:

Web site 1 A useful summary of the phyla which make up the animal kingdom.

Web site 2 Detailed information on classification, with an interactive classification activity.

Web site 3 Lots of descriptions of different mammal orders and species, with diagrams and assorted fascinating facts.

Web site 4 Information about the naming and classification of insects, with striking images.

** Nocturnal animals, 31, 54;
Social animals, 29, 54.*

FACTS AND LISTS

INFORMAL GROUPS

These are the main terms used to group animals by aspects of their lifestyles, such as what they eat and where they live.

Abyssal Living at great depths in the sea, e.g. gulper eels.

Demersal Living at the bottom of a lake or shallow sea, e.g. prawns.

Pelagic Living in the main body of a sea or lake, as opposed to the depths, e.g. whales.

Sessile Living things, such as barnacles, which are permanently fixed to the ground or an object.

Sedentary Staying mostly in one place, but not permanently attached, e.g. sea anemones.

Nocturnal Active at night and sleeping during the day, e.g. owls.

Diurnal Active during the day and sleeping at night, e.g. chimps.

Crepuscular Mostly active at dusk and dawn, e.g. desert foxes.

Predators Animals such as lions which kill and eat other animals (their **prey**). Bird predators, such as hawks, are called **raptors**.

Detritus feeders Animals such as earthworms which feed on decaying plant or animal matter.

Scavengers Large detritus feeders such as vultures, which feed on dead flesh.

Territorial Animals which hold and defend a territory (an area of land or water), either singly or in a group. Usually connected with attracting a mate and breeding.

Mutualists A pair of animals living closely together to the benefit of both, e.g. oxpeckers clean oxen by eating ticks off their bodies.

Parasites Animals or plants which live in or on other living things (their hosts) and feed off them.

Commensals A pair of living things which exist closely together; one benefits from this, while the other is unaffected. An example of this is house mice living wherever people are found.

Social or **colonial** Living together in groups. Social animals, such as lions, live together in fairly small groups. Colonial animals, such as ants, live in large groups where every member has its own role.

ANIMALS AND THEIR YOUNG

Here is a short list of facts and figures about animals and their young. This includes length of gestation period (the amount of time the mother is pregnant) and usual number of young born at once.

Animal	Gestation period	Number of young
Asian elephant	645 days	1
Indian rhinoceros	547 days	1
Giraffe	410 days	1
Whale	365 days	1
Horse	337 days	1
Chimpanzee	237 days	1
Sheep	148 days	1-2
Lion	108 days	1-2
Dog	61 days	3-6
Red kangaroo	35 days	1
Rabbit	31 days	10
House mouse	19 days	4-20
American opossum	13 days	10

AVERAGE ANIMAL LIFESPANS

Adult mayfly	12 hours
Common housefly	3 weeks
Monarch butterfly	1-2 years
Mole	3-4 years
Rat	4 years
European rabbit	Up to 5 years
European hedgehog	6 years
Two-toed sloth	8-12 years
Giant anteater	Up to 14 years
Koala	15-20 years
Giraffe	15-25 years
Zebra	20-30 years
Chimpanzee	30-40 years
Arabian camel	25-40 years
Rhinoceros	20-50 years
Hippopotamus	40-50 years
Killer whale	50-70 years
Asian elephant	70-75 years
Human	75-80 years
Fin whale	90 years
Tortoise	120 years

ENDANGERED ANIMALS

Listed here are some of the most endangered animals and their remaining numbers. These may increase if conservation schemes are successful.

Species	Numbers remaining worldwide	Reasons for endangered status
Black-footed ferret	Fewer than 1,000	Loss of prairie habitat, killing of prairie dogs (the ferrets' main food source), disease
Californian condor	Fewer than 40	Some wiped out by farmers who saw them as a threat to livestock. Many killed by lead poisoning from polluted environment
Giant panda	About 700	Habitat loss and food shortage
Golden lion tamarin	About 550 in the wild	Habitat loss
Hyacinth macaw	About 3,000	Captured for the pet trade, killed for their feathers
Kakapo	Approximately 60	Introduction of foreign predators into their natural habitat
Mountain gorilla	Approximately 600	Habitat loss, hunting
Northern right whale	About 350	Killed by boats and fishing nets
Siberian tiger	About 900	Habitat loss, hunted for body parts
Spectacled bear	Between 2,000 and 2,400	Habitat loss, hunting
White rhino	Fewer than 500	Habitat loss, hunted for its horn

USEFUL WEB SITES

Go to **www.usborne-quicklinks.com** and enter the keywords "science animals" for links to the following useful Web sites:

General animal sites

Web site 1 Find out about African Wildlife.

Web site 2 SeaWorld in Florida's searchable database of animal information.

Web site 3 Search for facts about many different kinds of animals.

Web site 4 News and information about Australian Wildlife.

Web site 5 Animal factfiles, news and more.

Web site 6 Official Web site of the Discovery Channel's Animal Planet, with videos, pictures, special features and more.

Web site 7 Animal videos, games, facts and links.

Web site 8 Lots of information about birdwatching and bird conservation.

Specific species

Web site 1 A very useful penguin resource.

Web site 2 Lots of facts about the five subspecies of tigers and the dangers they face.

Web site 3 Find out more about wolves.

Web site 4: Lots of fascinating facts about bears.

Web site 5: A useful elephant resource.

Web site 6: Pictures and facts about bears.

Conservation

Web site 1 Official Web site of the Rare Species Conservatory Foundation.

Web site 2 The Wildlife Preservation Trust International's site for kids.

Web site 3 Useful information about bat conservation and what you can do to help.

Web site 4 Lots of facts about rainforest animals and the dangers they face.

Web site 5 Videos of endangered species.

Web site 6 The kakapo is the world's most endangered parrot. Find out what is being done to save it.

Web site 7 Meet the primates in a real ape rescue centre.

Web site 8 Official Web site of the Royal Society for the Protection of Birds, a UK conservation organization.

Web site 9 Official Web site of the World Wide Fund for Nature.

Environmental issues

Web site 1 A global information source on endangered animals.

Web site 2 Official Web site of Friends of the Earth, an important environmental organization.

Web site 3 Official Web site of environmental campaign group Greenpeace.

Web site 4 An organization dedicated to oceanic conservation.

Web site 5 Explore environmental issues with Tiki the friendly penguin.

Web site 6 The Web site of an active environmental group, with lots of news.

Web site 7 Explore an online Earth science museum for information about the Earth and how its environment has changed over time.

Zoos

Web site 1 An online guide to the best zoos around the world.

Image galleries

Web site 1 Image gallery of the World Wide Fund for Nature, with pictures of birds, mammals, ocean life and people.

Web site 2 An image gallery of the Earth's vanishing animals.

Reference material

Web site 1 Fact Monster has answers to thousands of questions.

Web site 2 National Geographic magazine online, just for kids.

A-Z OF SCIENTIFIC TERMS

Abiotic Mineral or inorganic.
abyssal Living at great depths in the ocean.
aestivation A stage of some animals' life cycles when they enter a sleep-like state to survive drought.
albumen The white of a cleidoic egg. It provides the embryo with water and proteins, and supports the yolk.
alveoli Tiny sacs at the ends of bronchioles, where gases are exchanged between the lungs and the blood.
amphibians A class of cold-blooded, soft-skinned animals, which live both on land and in water, for example, frogs.
ampullae of Lorenzi Small chambers in a shark's head that allow it to detect the electrical pulses given off by other creatures.
anal fin A median fin projecting from behind a fish's anus.
annelids (**Annelida**) A phylum of worms with round, segmented bodies.
antennae (or **feelers**) Whip-like jointed structures on the heads of creatures such as insects and crustaceans, used for smelling, tasting and feeling.
arthropods (**Arthropoda**) A phylum of creatures with segmented bodies, jointed legs and an exoskeleton, for example, beetles and lobsters.
asexual reproduction Producing a new organism from a single parent.
autotrophic A term describing organisms such as plants, that make their own food from non-living materials. See also *photosynthesis*.

Bacteria A varied group of microscopic organisms without cell nuclei.
baleen (or **whalebone**) Frayed, horny plates in whales' mouths which they use to filter feed.
barbs Thin filaments branching from the central shaft of a feather.
barbules Tiny, hooked projections on the barbs of feathers, which lock together to join the barbs into a flat surface (called the **vane**).
bilateral symmetry A term describing the structure of an animal's body, in which each half is a mirror image of the other.
binary fission A form of asexual reproduction whereby a cell splits into identical halves.
binocular vision The ability of animals to see objects, using both eyes at the same time.
binomial system The system of giving organisms two-part names (see also *biological name*).

biological key A method of identifying the species of an organism by asking a series of questions about it, often shown as a tree diagram.
biological name A two-part Latin name used to classify organisms. The first part shows the genus; the second part shows the species within the genus (see *generic name*; *specific epithet*).
biomass The combined mass of all the living things in a habitat.
biomes The largest ecosystems into which the Earth can be divided.
bladder A balloon-like sac which stores urine until it is passed out of the body.
branchiae See *gills*.
bronchi Two thick tubes (each one a **bronchus**) into which the trachea divides, leading into the two lungs. Also the thinner tubes which branch off these first two.
bronchioles Tiny tubes in the lungs, which branch off the thinnest bronchi and end in alveoli.
budding A form of asexual reproduction, found in creatures such as hydras, which form growths called **buds** that break off to become new individuals.

Caecum A chamber found in the bodies of most herbivores, containing bacteria which break down cellulose.
carapace The shield-like hardened cuticle of animals such as crabs.
carbon cycle The process by which the element carbon enters the food chain through photosynthesis and returns to the atmosphere through respiration and decay.
carnassials Large, jagged teeth found in carnivores, used for slicing meat.
carnivores An order of mammals, including lions and foxes, with teeth specialized for eating flesh.
cartilage (or **gristle**) A tough, flexible tissue which, in most mammals, cushions joints and makes up such body parts as the ears and trachea. It forms the skeletons of young vertebrates, and of fish such as sharks.
caudal fin A fish's tail fin.
cell membrane A thin layer surrounding a cell's cytoplasm. In animal cells, it forms the outer layer.
cellulose A tough, glucose-based substance, from which plant cell walls are made.
centrioles Two X-shaped organelles that are important in cell division.
chaetae Bristles found on the bodies of some invertebrates, or on the end of their parapodia, which they use to move along.

chemoreceptors Body cells which sense the presence of certain chemicals.
chitin A sugar-based substance which forms the hard protective coverings of arthropods.
Chordates (**Chordata**) A phylum of animals with bodies supported by a stiff rod called a **notochord**.
cilia 1. Tiny hairs on the bodies of some microscopic animals which they flick back and forth to propel themselves. 2. Tiny hairs on the linings of the body organs of larger creatures.
ciliate A microscopic organism with external cilia.
circulatory system The interconnected network of arteries and veins that carries blood around an animal's body.
cirri Bristly limbs used for filter feeding by creatures such as barnacles.
classical taxonomy The classification of living things into five kingdoms: monera, protista, fungi, plants and animals. Each of these kingdoms has further subdivisions.
cleavage furrow A constriction around the middle of a cell that pinches it until it divides.
cleidoic egg A hard-shelled egg, laid by animals such as birds and reptiles, in which the embryo is fed by a food store called a **yolk** (see also *yolk sac*).
climax community The final, stable community in the process of ecological succession. It survives in its habitat as long as the environment remains stable.
clitellum A saddle-like body part on an earthworm.
cloaca A chamber in the body of some animals, such as birds, where waste is stored before being excreted.
Cnidarians (**Cnidaria**) A phylum of water creatures, such as jellyfish, whose sack-like bodies have a single opening.
cnidoblasts (or **thread cells**) Specialized cells on the tentacles of creatures such as sea anemones, used for seizing food.
coelom A type of perivisceral cavity that is contained by a peritoneum.
cold-blooded A term describing animals such as reptiles, that cannot control their internal temperature by body processes.
commensals Organisms living together where one benefits without affecting the other.
complete metamorphosis The type of metamorphosis in which the young form is very different from the adult.
compound eyes Eyes made up of many tiny lenses, such as those of insects. They produce **mosaic images**.

consumers All organisms above the trophic level of the producers (plants) in a food chain.

contour feathers The feathers that cover a bird's body, making a streamlined surface.

contractile vacuole A tiny sac in the body of a unicellular creature, which allows it to maintain its water balance.

crepuscular Active at dawn or dusk.

crop In birds, a thin-walled pouch which temporarily stores swallowed food.

cud See *ruminants*.

cuticle The protective, waterproof outer layer of the epidermis of many animals.

cytoplasm The gel-like substance inside a cell in which organelles are suspended.

Decomposers Tiny organisms, including bacteria and fungi, which break down dead animal and plant matter into chemicals in the soil.

demersal Living at the bottom of a lake or shallow sea.

dentate A term describing an animal with teeth.

denticles See *placoid scales*.

dermal scales Small, bony plates embedded in the skin of a fish.

dermis The thick, lower layer of skin beneath the epidermis.

detritus feeders Animals which feed on decaying organic matter.

diastema A gap between the front and cheek teeth of herbivores.

dichotomous key A biological key in which there are only two choices at each stage.

digestive system A system of organs that breaks down food into simpler substances.

digitigrade An animal, such as a dog, that walks on the underside of its toes.

diurnal Active in the daytime and sleeping at night.

dorsal fin The fin on a fish's back.

Ecdysis The process by which an arthropod sheds an outgrown cuticle and grows a new, larger one.

Echinoderms (Echinodermata) A phylum of sea creatures, such as starfish, with suckered feet and five-part bodies.

echo location A method of locating an object by detecting the return of sound waves bouncing off that object.

ecological niche The role of an animal in its community, including where it lives and what it eats.

ecological succession The way in which different communities replace each other as a habitat changes (see also *climax community; pioneer community*).

electroreception The ability of an organism to sense the electricity given off by itself or another organism.

elytra The hardened front wings of beetles and some bugs, which protect the fragile rear wings (used for flying).

endemic A term describing a plant, animal or disease which is found only in one place.

endoplasmic reticulum A series of channels which transport substances around a cell.

endoskeleton A hard, bony skeleton that supports an animal's body from the inside.

epidermis The outer layer of an animal's skin, sometimes coated.

epithelium Any tissue which forms a surface covering or cavity lining.

excretory organs Organs that deal with the removal of waste from the body.

exoskeleton A hard body covering which supports and protects the bodies of animals with no internal skeleton.

Fertilization The joining of male and female sex cells to form the first cell of a new individual.

filter feeding Feeding by sieving tiny plants or animals out of water.

flagellae Long, fine threads on the bodies of some microscopic animals which they lash to and fro in order to propel themselves.

flagellate A term which describes an organism with flagellae.

flame cells Cells through which waste passes into protonephridia.

Flatworms (also known as **Platyhelminthes**) A phylum of worms with flat, unsegmented bodies.

food chain A series of living things, each one eaten by the next in line.

food web A series of linked food chains.

fragmentation A form of asexual reproduction in a few animals, such as some worms, whereby new individuals can form from fragmented parts of one animal.

fungi Plant-like organisms that cannot make their own food, so feed on dead or living plant or animal matter.

Gaseous exchange The term which describes the movement of gases in and out of an organism's body.

generic name The first part of a biological name, showing an organism's genus.

genes The pairs of chemical instructions which together give all the information needed to build a living thing. See also *heredity*.

genus (pl. **genera**) A subdivision in classical taxonomy. Genera are groups of species.

gestation period The length of time a baby mammal spends in the womb before birth.

gills (or **branchiae**) The respiratory organs of most water creatures.

gill slits Openings in the sides of water creatures, such as fish, which allow water to pass across the gills and out of the body.

gizzard In birds, a thick-walled pouch which contains muscular ridges and small stones for grinding up solid food.

Golgi complex A specialized area of the endoplasmic reticulum which collects and distributes the substances made in a cell.

Haemocoel A type of perivisceral cavity which contains blood, and is connected to the circulatory system.

haltères The tiny back wings of flies, modified for balancing the body in flight.

herbivore An animal that eats plants.

heredity The passing on of characteristics, or **traits**, from one generation to the next, through genes. A gene for each trait is passed to an offspring from each parent.

hermaphrodite An organism that has both male and female sex cells.

heterotrophic A term describing organisms such as animals, that depend on other living things for food.

hexapod A six-legged animal.

hibernation A stage of some animals' life cycles when they enter a sleep-like state to survive the winter cold.

homeostasis An organism's natural regulation of its internal conditions, such as temperature and chemical balance.

hotspot An area containing large numbers of endemic species.

hydrostatic skeleton A system which supports body structure, and sometimes movement, by the working of muscles in the body wall against the pressurized fluid in a perivisceral cavity.

hyponome A funnel-shaped tube on the bodies of animals such as octopuses, from which they shoot jets of water to propel themselves.

hypopharynx A type of tongue in some insects, used for sucking up liquids.

Imago The adult form of an insect.

incomplete fission A form of multiple fission, found in creatures such as corals, where the new individuals stay joined together.

incomplete metamorphosis The type of metamorphosis in which the young look similar to the adults.

internal respiration The process by which animals and plants use oxygen to break down their food, producing energy and releasing carbon dioxide.

invertebrate An animal without a backbone.

Jacobson's organs Two pits in the roof of a snake's mouth, used for smelling and tasting.

Keel The extension of a bird's breastbone to which the wing muscles are attached.

keratin A waterproof protein of which animal horns, hair, nails and feathers are mostly made.

kidneys Excretory organs which remove waste from the blood and regulate the body's fluid levels.

Labium An insect's lower lip.

labrum An insect's hinged upper lip.

larva An early stage of development of many kinds of animal, e.g. a caterpillar.

lateral lines Two water-filled tube-like channels in the bodies of fish, and some amphibians, which help them to detect vibrations made by other animals in the water.

lateral vision The field of vision of an animal with eyes on the sides of its head.

liver A large organ that breaks down food substances, filters out some poisons, and stores carbohydrates, minerals and vitamins.

locomotion The process by which animals move around.

lysosomes Organelles containing powerful enzymes which destroy bacteria invading a cell.

Malpighian tubules Excretory tubes in arthropods which remove liquid waste from the haemocoel.

mammary glands Glands in a female mammal which produce milk for the young.

mandible 1. An insect mouthpart, used for gripping or biting. 2. A mammal's jawbone.

mass extinctions Five points in Earth's ancient past when huge numbers of living things died out in a very short time.

maxillae Insect mouthparts used to push food into the mouth.

median fins Fins that lie in a line down the middle of a fish's back or belly.

metameres The near-identical segments into which the bodies of some animals, such as worms, are divided.

metamorphosis A stage in some animals' life cycles when their bodies undergo a change, such as when a caterpillar turns into a butterfly or a tadpole turns into a frog.

migration A stage in some animals' life cycles when they travel a long distance to find food or to mate.

mimicry The colouration of some animals to resemble more dangerous animals, serving to defend them against predators.

mitochondria Rod-shaped organelles which act as a cell's powerhouses, breaking down simple substances to provide energy.

molluscs (Mollusca) A phylum of soft-bodied creatures which mostly have shells, for example, snails.

Monera Microscopic organisms, such as bacteria, whose cells have no nuclei.

multiple fission Repeated, constant binary fission.

mutualists Organisms that benefit each other by living closely together.

Natural selection The process whereby individuals with features which are best suited to their environment are more likely to survive and produce young. The young then inherit the parents' favourable features.

nematocyst A poisonous thread, coiled inside a cnidoblast, which shoots out to paralyse prey.

nematodes (Nematoda) A phylum of long, thin, round worms with unsegmented bodies.

nephridiopores Tiny holes at the ends of protonephridia through which waste is ejected.

nitrates A group of salts which occur naturally and are essential to plant growth.

nitrogen cycle The natural process by which nitrogen gas is converted into nitrates in the soil, used by plants, and returned again to the air.

nocturnal A term describing animals which are mostly active at night.

notochord See *chordates*.

nuclear membrane The double-layered outer skin of a cell's nucleus.

nuclear pores Holes in the nuclear membrane which allow substances to pass between the cytoplasm and nucleus.

nucleolus An organelle in a cell's nucleus which produces the ingredients of ribosomes.

nucleus The part of a cell that controls all of its processes.

nymphs The young forms of insects such as locusts, that undergo incomplete metamorphosis.

Omnivores Animals that eat both plants and other animals.

operculum A flap which covers the gills in bony fish.

organelle Any of the small parts in the cytoplasm of a cell. Different types of organelle have different functions.

oviparous Egg-laying.

ovum The female sex cell of an animal.

Paired fins Pairs of fins that stick out of the sides of a fish's body.

palps Insect mouthparts used to touch, taste and smell food.

parapodia Pairs of jointless projections on the sides of animals such as bristleworms, which they flex to swim around and burrow.

parasite An organism which lives and feeds upon another. It may harm its host.

parthenogenesis Production of new individuals from sex cells, without fertilization having taken place.

pectoral fins Paired shoulder fins that project from just behind a fish's gills.

pectoralis muscles The breast muscles. Highly developed in birds, for use in flight.

pelagic Living in the main body of a sea or lake.

pelvic fins Paired fins that project from a fish's pelvic region.

peritoneum A thin membrane which lines the body wall surrounding a coelom.

perivisceral cavity A fluid-filled body cavity cushioning the internal organs in most animals.

phagocytosis The process by which a unicellular organism digests food by changing its shape to engulf it. Some white blood cells also act in this way to destroy germs.

pheromone A chemical released by an animal which sends a message to others, for example, to attract a mate.

photoreceptors Light-sensitive cells, such as those found in the eyes.

photosynthesis The process by which plants use energy from sunlight to power the production of food (glucose) from water and carbon dioxide.

phylum A subdivision in classical taxonomy. Phyla are the next divisions after the main five kingdoms.

pinna An external ear flap.

pioneer community The first community in the process of ecological succession.

pit organ An organ on a snake's head which allows it to detect its prey's body heat from a distance.

placenta An organ in the womb that provides an unborn mammal with food and oxygen from its mother during gestation.

placoid scales (or **denticles**) Sharp, backward-pointing scales which stick out of the skin of fish such as sharks.

plantigrade An animal, such as a bear, that walks on the underside of its whole foot.

predators Animals which kill other animals (their prey) for food.

prehensile A term describing part of an animal which is specially adapted for grasping.

proboscis A long feeding tube, in insects such as butterflies, formed from fused maxillae.

producers Organisms at the lowest trophic level of a food chain, that is, plants, which provide energy for all those above them.

protective adaptations Features developed through natural selection which help to protect organisms from damage or danger.

Protista A kingdom of single-celled organisms which combine features of both plants and animals.

protonephridia Waste-collecting tubes found in animals such as simple worms.

protoplasm The matter of which cells are made, consisting of the cell membrane, nucleus and cytoplasm.

pseudopodia Extensions formed temporarily from the bodies of single-celled animals to enable locomotion or feeding.

pupa A stage of metamorphosis when an insect is protected by a hard case.

Radial symmetry A term describing the structure of an animal that can be divided into identical halves by two or more lines of symmetry radiating from a central point.

radula A mollusc's rough tongue, used for scraping plant matter into the mouth.

raptors Birds which are predators.

receptors Sensitive cells which send information about an animal's surroundings to its brain.

regeneration The ability to regrow parts of the body which have been broken off.

respiration (also **external respiration** or **breathing**) The process of taking in oxygen and giving out carbon dioxide. See also *internal respiration*.

respiratory organs Organs concerned with breathing, for example, lungs or gills.

ribosomes Tiny round organelles that help to produce proteins in a cell.

ruminant A mammal, such as a cow or camel, which has even-toed hooves, four digestive chambers, and chews the **cud** (regurgitated, semi-digested food).

Scavengers Animals which eat the dead flesh of other creatures.

sclerites The hard sections of an arthropod's cuticle, which are connected by flexible membranes.

scuta (sing. **scute**) Hard protective plates covering the bodies of some animals, such as armadillos.

sedentary A term describing animals that stay mostly in one place, for example sea anemones.

septum A wall of muscle tissue separating one metamere from the next.

sessile A term describing animals which are permanently fixed in one place, for example barnacles.

setae Bristles found on the bodies of many invertebrates, used to sense air movement.

sexual reproduction Reproduction which involves joining male and female sex cells.

sign stimulus A visual display that triggers a set response from another creature, for example, when a robin displays its red breast to show aggression.

siphon A tube that carries water to or from the gills in many simple water creatures. An **inhalant siphon** carries water to the gills; an **exhalant siphon** carries it away.

spawn The many tiny, soft eggs laid by most fish and amphibians.

specialization The developed suitability of cells and organisms for a particular function, environment or way of life.

species A group of organisms that can interbreed with each other.

specific epithet The second part of a biological name, which shows an organism's species.

sperm The male sex cells of an animal.

spiracles Small holes along the sides of insects' bodies, through which they breathe.

stance A term describing how an animal stands.

statocyst An organ of balance, found in creatures such as jellyfish, made up of a sac filled with receptors and tiny grains called **statoliths**.

stereoscopic vision The type of vision in which each eye gives a slightly different view, allowing the brain to form a 3D image.

stridulation The rubbing together of body parts to produce a shrill noise, as is done by crickets to attract a mate.

swim bladder An inflatable sac in the body of a bony fish. The fish varies the amount of air in the swim bladder to make its body rise or sink.

syrinx The part of a bird's windpipe with which it sings.

Tactile receptors Cells on animals' bodies which allow them to detect touch.

tagmata Segments that make up the body regions (head, thorax and abdomen) of animals such as insects. They are not divided by internal walls.

tapetum A reflective layer at the back of the eyes of nocturnal animals, and some fish, which collects light to help them to see.

taxonomic rank A named level in classification, e.g. phylum.

taxon A named group in classification, e.g. Arthropoda.

tentacles Long, flexible limbs found on many molluscs and some sea creatures. They are often used for grasping and feeling.

terrestrial animals Animals that live mostly on land.

thermoregulation The process by which an animal keeps its body at the right temperature.

thread cells See *cnidoblasts*.

trachea (or **windpipe**) The respiratory tube in birds, reptiles and mammals, through which air flows into the lungs and carbon dioxide is breathed out.

tracheae The tiny tubes in an insect's body, leading from the spiracles to the tracheoles.

tracheoles Very tiny tubes which carry gases to and from the cells in an insect's body.

traits See *heredity*.

trophic level The position of an organism within a food chain.

tundra A biome with harsh winds and low temperatures. Its underground soil is always frozen, so it has no trees.

tympanal organ A simple hearing organ found in animals such as frogs, consisting of a tympanum on the body surface which passes vibrations into an air sac containing receptors.

tympanum A thin layer of tissue found in most land animals, which enables them to hear by vibrating in response to sound waves.

Unguligrade An animal that walks upon hooves at its toe-tips, such as a horse.

urea A waste substance produced in the liver from the breakdown of amino acids.

uric acid A weak organic acid excreted as solid waste by some animals, such as reptiles and birds.

urine A waste substance produced by the kidneys, made of urea, water and toxic salts.

uterus See *womb*.

Vacuole A fluid-filled sac inside a cell. Animal cell vacuoles are small and temporary.

vane See *barbules*.

vertebrate An animal with a backbone.

vibrissae (or **whiskers**) Long, stiff hairs on an animal's face, that are sensitive to touch.

viruses Strands of a chemical called **DNA** (or a related chemical called **RNA**) in a protective coat. They cannot live on their own, but invade living cells and reproduce, often causing diseases such as colds.

viviparous A term describing animals which give birth to live young.

Warm-blooded A term describing animals which can keep their internal temperature constant under most conditions.

water cycle The natural process by which water is recycled between the Earth, the atmosphere and living things.

whalebone (See *baleen*).

womb (or **uterus**) A sac inside the body of a female mammal, in which the young grows.

Yolk sac A sac in a cleidoic egg that contains food, called **yolk**, rich in phosphorus and fat, which nourishes the embryo.

TEST YOURSELF

1. Protoplasm consists of
A. the nucleus
B. the nucleus and cytoplasm
C. the nucleus, cytoplasm and cell
   membrane *(Page 9)*

2. The liver is
A. a complex tissue
B. an organ
C. a body system *(Page 9)*

3. Most animals which actively move
about are
A. asymmetrical
B. radially symmetrical
C. bilaterally symmetrical *(Page 11)*

4. The skeleton of an insect is
A. a hydrostatic skeleton
B. an exoskeleton
C. an endoskeleton *(Page 11)*

5. Hedgehog spikes are made of
A. keratin
B. chitin
C. bone *(Page 12)*

6. A swim bladder can be found in
A. fish with cartilage skeletons
B. some fish with bone skeletons
C. all fish *(Page 14)*

7. Most beetles
A. cannot fly
B. fly by flapping both pairs of wings
C. fly by flapping one pair of
   wings *(Page 17)*

8. Dogs walk on
A. the underside of the whole foot
B. the undersides of the toes
C. the tips of the toes *(Page 19)*

9. Carnassial teeth are found in
A. herbivores
B. omnivores
C. carnivores *(Page 22)*

10. Animals which eat both plants
and other animals are called
A. omnivores
B. carnivores
C. herbivores *(Page 22)*

11. In a bird, food is stored in the
A. crop
B. gizzard
C. cloaca *(Page 23)*

12. Adult insects breathe using
A. gills
B. lungs
C. tracheae *(Page 25)*

13. Homeostasis is
A. keeping a constant body
   temperature
B. keeping a constant internal
   environment
C. keeping the external environment
   constant *(Page 26)*

14. Mimicry involves
A. copying the behaviour of another
   animal
B. copying the warning colours of
   another animal
C. copying another animal's scent
   (Page 28)

15. Some snakes detect the body
heat of their prey with
A. antennae
B. lateral lines
C. pit organs *(Page 33)*

16. The body of a hermaphrodite
animal contains
A. only female sex cells
B. both male and female sex cells
C. only male sex cells *(Page 35)*

17. In cleidoic eggs the young are
A. fed by a yolk
B. called spawn
C. inside the mother *(Page 37)*

18. A locust hopper is a stage of
A. complete metamorphosis
B. incomplete metamorphosis
C. migration *(Pages 38-39)*

19. A habitat is
A. the natural home for plants and
   animals
B. a group of animals
C. too cold to support life *(Page 40)*

20. An ecological niche can support
A. one animal species
B. two animal species
C. several animal species *(Page 40)*

21. The largest ecosystems are
A. habitats
B. communities
C. biomes *(Page 41)*

22. An organism which eats
another organism is
A. autotrophic
B. heterotrophic
C. parasitic *(Page 42)*

23. At the second trophic level, an
animal is a
A. producer
B. primary consumer
C. secondary consumer *(Page 42)*

24. An organism which breaks
down dead plant and animal
matter is a
A. decomposer
B. consumer
C. producer *(Page 42)*

25. A trophic level has
A. fewer consumers than the level
   below
B. more consumers than the level
   below
C. the same number of consumers
   as all other levels
   (Page 42)

26. The abiotic parts of an
environment are made up of
A. living or organic matter
B. mineral or inorganic matter
C. dead matter *(Page 43)*

27. Endemic species of animals
are
A. found in many different places
B. found in only one place
C. found only on islands *(Page 47)*

28. The largest taxonomic ranks
after kingdoms are
A. orders
B. classes
C. phyla *(Page 51)*

29. Biological names of living
organisms are in
A. Greek
B. Latin
C. English *(Page 53)*

30. Animals which live close
together and both gain from the
situation are
A. mutualists
B. commensals
C. parasites *(Page 54)*

Answers

1.C 2.B 3.C 4.B 5.A 6.B 7.C 8.B 9.C 10.A 11.A 12.C 13.B 14.B 15.C 16.B 17.A 18.B 19.A 20.A 21.C 22.B 23.B 24.A 25.A 26.B 27.B 28.C 29.B 30.A

INDEX

You will find the main explanations of terms in the index on the pages shown in bold type. It may be useful to look at the other pages for further information.

A

abdomen **10**
abiotic 44, 56
abomasum 23
abyssal 56
  animals 54
aestivation **39**, 56
albumen **37**, 56
alveoli **25**, 56
ammonia 44
amoeba 10, 14, 34
amphibians 48, **52**, **56**
  breathing in **25**
  homeostasis in **36**, 37
ampullae of Lorenzi **33**, 56
anal fins 15, 56
animal kingdom **52**
annelids **52**, 56
antennae **32**, 56
armadillo 12
arthropods 27, **52**, 56
asexual reproduction **34**, 35, 56
autotrophic 42, 56

B

babies **37**
background rate of extinction **46**
bacteria 23, 42, 44, 48, **51**, 56
balance **30**
baleen (whalebone) 20, 56
barbs **16**, 56
barbules **16**, 56
beaks **21**
bee dances **29**
bilateral symmetry **11**, 56
binary fission **34**, 56
binocular vision **31**, 56
binomial system **53**, 56
biological
  keys **50**, 56
  names **53**, 56
biomass **43**, 56
biomes **41**, 56
biped **19**
birds 27, 37, 45, 48, **52**
  flight in **16**
  digestion in **23**
  communication in **28**
  migration of 33, **39**
bladder **27**, 56
body
  coverings **12-13**
  structure **10-11**

bones (of birds) **16**
branchiae **24**, 56
breathing **24-25**, 56
bristleworm 14
bronchi **25**, 56
bronchioles **25**, 56
budding **34**, 56
burning fuels 45

C

caecum **23**, 56
camouflage **49**
canines
  dog family **52**
  teeth **22**
carapace **12**, 56
carbon 44
  cycle **44**, 56
  dioxide 42
carnassials **22**, 56
carnivores 56
  eating habits **22**, 42
  order 52
cartilage **11**, 56
cartilaginous fish 11
caudal fins 15, 56
cells **8-9**
cell
  division **9**
  membrane **8**, 56
cellulose 23, 56
centrioles **8**, 56
chaetae 14, 56
chemoreceptors **33**, 56
chitin 12, 56
chordates 52, 56
cilia **14**, 56
ciliates **14**, 56
circulatory system 9, 56
cirri 20, 56
class 51
classical taxonomy **51**, 56
classification **50-53**
cleavage furrow 9, 56
cleidoic eggs **37**, 56
climax community **40**, 56
clitellum **35**, 56
cloaca **23**, 56
clone **34**
cnidarians **20**, 52, 56
cnidoblasts **20**, 56
coelom **11**, 56
cold-blooded **26**, 56
columnar epithelial cells **9**
commensals **53**, 56
communication **28-29**
community **40**
complete metamorphosis **38**, 56
compound eyes **31**, 56
colonial animals **54**
colouration, **28**
coniferous forests **41**
conservation **46-47**
consumers **42**, 57
contour feathers **16**, 57

contractile vacuole **27**, 57
corals 34, 47
courtship ritual **36**
crawling **18**
crepuscular **57**
crop (in birds) **23**, 57
cud 23, 57
cuticle **12**, 57
cytoplasm **8**, 14, 57

D

Darwin, Charles 49
daughter cell 9, **34**
deciduous forests **41**
decomposers 42, **57**
demersal 57
  animals **54**
dentate **22**, 57
denticles **13**, 57
dermal scales **13**, 57
dermis **13**, 57
deserts **41**
detritus feeders 54, **57**
diastema **22**, 57
dichotomous key **50**, 57
digestion **23**
digestive system 9, **23**, 57
digitigrade **19**, 57
diurnal **54**, 57
dominant animals 29
dormancy 39
dorsal fins **15**, 57
dragonfly 17

E

eardrum **30**
ears **30**
earthworm **10**, 18
ecdysis **12**, 57
echinoderms 52, 57
echo location **30**, 57
ecological
  niches **40**, 57
  succession **40**, 57
ecology **40-41**
ecosystem **40**, 47
edentates 20
eggs (ova) **37**
electroreception **33**, 57
elytra **17**, 57
embryo **36**
endangered species 45, **46**, 55
endemic **47**, 57
endoplasmic reticulum **8**, 57
endoskeleton **11**, 57
energy **42-43**
environment **40**, 41
epidermis **13**, 57
epithelium **9**, 57
euglena 51
evolution **48-49**
excretory organs 26, **27**, 57
exhalant siphons **24**, 59 (siphons)
exoskeletons **11**, 12, 57

external
  fertilization **36**
  gills **24**
  respiration 59 (respiration)
extinction **46**, 49
eyes **31**

F

families **51**
feathers **16**
feelers **32**, 56 (antennae)
felines **52**
fertilization **35**, 57
filter feeding **20**, 57
fins (of a fish) 14, **15**
fish 45, 48, **52**
  scales of 13
  movement in **15**
  breathing in 24
  senses of 33
  reproduction in 36-37
  migration of 39
flagellae **14**, 57
flagellate **14**, 57
flame cells **27**, 57
flatworms 52, 57
flight**16-17**
  feathers **16**
flippers 14, **15**
food **42-43**
  chains **42**, 45, 57
  webs **43**, 57
fossils **48**
fragmentation **34**, 57
frogs 9
  breathing in 24
  reproduction in 36, **38**
frogspawn 36, **37**
fry (salmon) 39
fungi 42, 44, **51**, 57

G

gaseous exchange **24**, 57
generic names **53**, 57
genes 57
genus (See *genera*)
genera (sing. genus) **51**, 52-53, 57
gestation periods 54, 57
gills 57
gill slits 57
giraffes 40, 53
gizzard 57
golden lion tamarin, 47
Golgi complex **57**
gristle 56 (cartilage)

H

habitats **40**, 47
haemocoel **11**, 57
haltères **30**, 57
hearing **30**
herbivores **22**, 42, 57
hermaphrodites **35**, 57
heterotrophic **42**, 57

hexapods **19**, 57
hibernation **39**, 57
homeostasis **26-27**, 57
hopper 38
host 53
hotspots **47**, 57
hydra 34
hydrostatic skeletons **11**, 57
hyponomes **14**, 57
hypopharynx 21, 57

I

imago 38, 57
incisors **22**
incomplete
  fission **34**, 57
  metamorphosis **38**, 57
inhalant siphons 24, 59 (siphon)
insecticides **45**
insects 29, 35, 40, 48, 50
  body structure of **10**
  flight in 17
  movement in 19
  breathing in 25
  sight in 31
  life cycles of 38
interdependence **43**
internal
  fertilization **36**
  gills **24**
  respiration 57
invertebrates **32**, 57

J

Jacobson's organ **33**, 57

K

keel 16, 58
keratin 13, 58
kidneys 27, 58
kingdoms 51

L

labium 21, 58
labrum 21, 58
larvae **38**, 58
lateral
  lines **33**, 58
  vision **31**, 58
leaping 19
life cycles **38-39**
lifespans **54**
liver **27**, 58
locomotion **14-19**, 58
looping (in caterpillars) **18**
lungs **25**
lysosomes 8, 58

M

malpighian tubules **27**, 58
mammals 48, 52
mammary glands **37**, 58

mandibles **21**, 58
maquis 41
mass extinctions **49**, 58
mating **36**
maxillae 21, 58
median fins **15**, 58
metameres **10**, 58
metameric segmentation **10**
metamorphosis **38**, 58
migration 33, **39**, 58
mimicry **28**, 58
mitochondria 8, 58
molars **22**
molluscs 52, 58
monera **51**, 58
mosaic images **31**, 56 (compound eyes)
mountains **41**
multicellular 10
multiple fission **34**, 58
mutualists 53, **54**, 58
myriapods **19**

N

natural selection **49**, 58
nature reserves **46**
nematocysts **20**, 58
nematodes 52, 58
nephridiopores 27, 58
nitrates **44**, 58
nitrogen **44**
  cycle **44**, 58
nocturnal 58
  animals **31**, 54
notochords 52, 58
nuclear
  membrane **8**, 58
  pores **8**, 58
nucleolus **8**, 58
nucleus **8-9**, 58
nymphs **38**, 58

O

oceans **41**
octopus 14, 32
omasum 23
omnivores **22**, 58
operculum **24**, 58
order 51, 52
organ **9**
organelles 8, 58
organism 9
ossicles **30**
ova (sing. ovum) **36**, 58 (ovum)
overfishing **45**
oviparous **37**, 58
ovum (See *ova*)
owl 16, 23

P

paired fins **15**, 58
palps 21, 33, 58
panda 47
Paramecium 14, 27, 34
parapodia **14**, 58

parasites **53**, 54, 58
parthenogenesis **35**, 58
pectoral fins 15, 58
pectoralis muscles 16, 58
pelagic 58
   animals **54**
pellet **23**
pelvic fins 15, 58
penis 36
peritoneum **11**, 58
perivisceral cavities **11**, 58
permanent teeth **22**
phagocytosis **20**, 58
pheromones **29**, 36, 58
photoreceptors **31**, 58
phylum **51**, 58
pinna 30, 58
pioneer community **40**, 58
pit organ 33, 58
placenta 37, 58
placoid scales **13**, 58
plantigrade **19**, 58
polar climate **41**
pollution **45**
predators 54, 58
prehensile 18, 58
prehistoric life **48-49**
premolars **22**
primary consumer **42**
primates 37, **52**
   movement in 18
   teeth of 22
   senses of 31
proboscis **21**, 58
producers **42**, 58
protective adaptations **49**, 58
proteins 8, 44
protista 51, 58
protonephridia **27**, 59
protoplasm 8, 59
pseudopodia **14**, 59
pupa **38**, 59
pupil **31**
pyramid
   of biomass **43**
   of numbers **42**

Q

quadruped **19**
quills 13

R

radial symmetry **11**, 59
radula 20, 59
raptors **54**, 59
rays (fish fins) **15**
receptors **30**, 59
regeneration **34**, 59
remiges (flight feathers) **16**
renal
   arteries **27**
   veins **27**
reproduction **34-37**
reptiles **26**, 42, 48, 49, 52
respiration 59

respiratory organs **24**, 59
reticulum 23
ribosomes 8, 59
rodents 52
rumen 23
ruminants **23**, 59

S

scales **13**
scavengers 54, 59
sclerites **12**, 59
scrublands 41
scuta **12**, 18, 59
sea anemone 11
secondary consumer (food chain) **42**
sedentary 59
   animals 54
segmented bodies **10**
senses **30-31**
septum 10, 59
sessile 54, 59
setae **32**, 59
sex cells **35**
sexual reproduction 35, **36-37**, 59
sharks 11
   scales of 13
   teeth of 22
   breathing in 24
   senses of 33
shell (mollusc) **12**
sight (See *vision*)
sign stimulus **28**, 59
siphons **24**, 59
skeletons **11**
slow breeders **47**
smell **33**
snakes 17, 18, 33
social animals **29**, 54
sound waves **30**
spawn **37**, 59
specialization **9**, 59
species 51, **52**, 59
specific epithets **53**, 59
sperm **36**, 59
spiracles **25**, 59
stance **19**, 59
statocysts **30**, 59
statoliths **30**, 59 (statocyst)
stereoscopic vision **31**
stridulation **29**, 59
sub-kingdoms 51
subordinates **29**
sub-phyla 51
succession (ecological) **40**
suckling **37**
support (body structure) **12-13**
sweat 26
swim bladder **15**, 59
swinging (primates) **18**
syrinx 29, 59
system (organs) 9

T

tactile receptors **32**, 59
tadpoles **38**, 24

tagmata 10, 59
tapetum **31**, 59
taste 33
taxonomic ranks (taxa) **51**, 59
teeth **22**
temperate grasslands **41**
temperature control **26**
tentacles **32**, 59
terrestrial animals **18-19**, 59
territorial animals 54
thermoregulation **26**, 59
thorax 10
thread cells **20**, 59
threatened species **46**
tissue (animal) 9
tortoise 12
touch **32**, 33
tracheae **25**, 59
tracheoles **25**, 59
traits 35, **59**
trichomonas 14
trophic levels **42**, 59
tropical
   grasslands **41**
   rainforests 41, **47**
tundra **41**, 49
tympanal organ **30**, 59
tympanum **30**, 59

U

unguligrade **19**, 59
unicellular **10**
urea **27**, 59
uric acid **27**, 59
urine **27**, 59
uterus (womb) **37**, 59

V

vacuoles (in cells) 8, **20**, 27, 59
vanes **16**, 59
ventral fins 15, 59
vertebrates 32, 59
vibrissae **32**, 59
viruses 51, **59**
vision **31**
viviparous **37**, 59

W

warm-blooded **26**, 59
water cycle **44**, 59
whiskers **32**, 59 (vibrissae)
windpipe 25, 59 (trachea)
wings **16**
womb **37**, 59
worms 11, 50, **52**
   body structure of 10
   reproduction in 34-35

Y

yolk **37**, 59
   sac **37**, 59

ACKNOWLEDGEMENTS

PHOTO CREDITS
(t = top, m = middle, b = bottom, l = left, r = right)

Corbis: 14-15 (t) Stephen Frink; **16-17** (main) David A. Northcott; **18-19** (b) Tom Brakefield; **22** (t) Michael Lewis; **24-25** (t) Amos Nachoum; **26-27** (main) W. Perry Conway; **28** (bl) Jim Zuckerman; **30** (t) Susan Middleton & David Liischwager; **31** (r) W. Perry Conway; **32** (bl) Stuart Westmorland; **34** (tr) Lester V. Bergman, (bl) Robert Yin; **35** (main) Robert Pickett; **38-39** (main) Yann Arthus-Bertrand; **40-41** (b) Kennan Ward; **42** Peter Johnson; **45** (b) Jim Sugar Photography; **46-47** (main) Annie Griffiths Belt; **48** (t) James L. Amos.
© **Digital Vision: cover**; **1**; **2-3**; **4-5**; **6-7**; **13** (tl); **19** (tl); **33** (ml); **45** (l); **46** (l); **47** (l), (bl); **53** (m), (b).
Bruce Coleman: **21** (t) John Cancalosi; **NHPA 22** (b), **Planet Earth Pictures 36** (tr).
Science Photo Library: **8-9** (t) Dr Yorgos Nikas; **51** (b) UDSA.
Still Pictures: **26** (b) John Cancalosi.
Telegraph Colour Library: **13** (b); **32-33** (main); **36** (b),
Undersea Research Programme (NURP): **10-11** (t).

ILLUSTRATORS
Simone Abel, Sophie Allington, Jane Andrews, Rex Archer, Paul Bambrick, Jeremy Banks, Andrew Beckett, Joyce Bee, Stephen Bennett, Roland Berry, Gary Bines, Isabel Bowring, Trevor Boyer, John Brettoner, Gerry Browne, Peter Bull, Hilary Burn, Andy Burton, Terry Callcut, Kuo Kang Chen, Stephen Conlin, Sydney Cornfield, Dan Courtney, Steve Cross, Gordon Davies, Peter Dennis, Richard Draper, Brin Edwards, John Francis, Mark Franklin, Peter Geissler, Nick Gibbard, William Giles, Mick Gillah, David Goldston, Peter Goodwin, Jeremy Gower, Teri Gower, Terry Hadler, Alan Harris, Nick Hawken, Nicholas Hewetson, Christine Howes, John Hutchinson, Ian Jackson, Hans Jessen, Karen Johnson, Richard Johnson, Elaine Keenan, Aziz Khan, Stephen Kirk, Richard Lewington, Brian Lewis, Jason Lewis, Steve Lings, Rachel Lockwood, Kevin Lyles, Chris Lyon, Kevin Maddison, Janos Marffy, Andy Martin, Josephine Martin, Rob McCaig, Joseph McEwan, David McGrail, Malcolm McGregor, Dee McLean, Annabel Milne, Robert Morton, Paddy Mounter, Louise Nevet, Martin Newton, Louise Nixon, Steve Page, Justine Peek, Maurice Pledger, Mick Posen, Russell Punter, Barry Raynor, Mark Roberts, Michael Roffe, Michelle Ross, Simon Roulstone, Graham Round, Michael Saunders, John Scorey, John Shackell, Chris Shields, David Slinn, Graham Smith, Guy Smith, Peter Stebbing, Ian Stephen, Sue Stitt, Stuart Trotter, Robert Walster, Craig Warwick, Ross Watton, Phil Weare, Hans Wiborg-Jenssen, Sean Wilkinson, Gerald Wood, David Wright, Nigel Wright.